GREEK
COOKING

INTERNATIONAL GOURMET

GREEK
COOKING

Pamela Westland

AEGEAN SEA

ATHENS

WARD LOCK

First published in paperback in Great Britain in 1990 by
Ward Lock Limited, Artillery House, Artillery Row,
London SW1P 1RT, a Cassell Company.

*Overleaf: 'Spoon' sweets such as these (page 92)
can be made from almost any small fruit and
preserved in jars*

Text filmset in Garamond Original by
M & R Computerised Typesetting Ltd.,
Grimsby.

Printed and bound in Portugal by Resopal.

British Library Cataloguing in Publication Data

Westland, Pamela
Greek cooking.
1. Cookery, Greece
I. Title
641.59495   TX723.5.G8

ISBN 0–7063–6864–9

Acknowledgements
Photography by James Murphy
Home Economist – Ricky Turner
Stylist – Sarah Wiley
Line drawings by Lorraine Harrison

Notes
It is important to follow **either** the metric
or the imperial measures when using the
recipes in this book. Do not use a
combination of measures.

CONTENTS

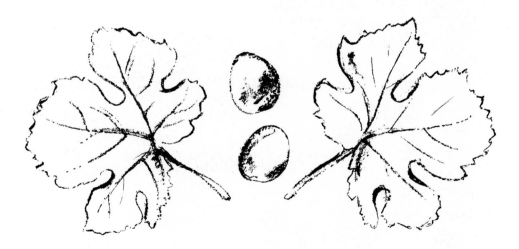

INTRODUCTION

Not long ago I had my first consultation with a clairvoyant. Instead of coming out with the conventional 'I see a dark stranger' type of prediction he announced, dramatically and somewhat surprisingly, 'I see another country.' Using a highly emotive phrase, he told me that this other country – no prizes for guessing that it had to be Greece – was more than home to me and always 'fitted me like a comfortable old coat'.

He described the terrain and architecture in detail, the barren mountains, the fertile valleys, the thousands of fascinating islands, the Venetian houses and the whitewashed streets. Warming to his theme he described the national cuisine down to the last mouth-watering detail, the spit-roast meat, the grilled sea-fresh fish, the herbs and the sticky pastries. And he eulogised about the people, using a phrase that I myself would unhesitatingly apply: the friendliest, most hospitable in the world.

'It is strange,' he concluded. 'You have such a high regard for this country and everything about it. Yet you never feel the least bit sad when the time comes to leave it. That must be a measure of your confidence and sense of belonging.'

So that's it. My only excuse for writing this book. No parental ties, no long-shared heritage, no childhood memories to draw on. Just a fellow feeling that grows stronger each time that I am able to go to Greece – once or twice a year, for short family holidays – and an appreciation of the food that, I have to admit, far transcends professional interest.

To my mind, Greek cooking is all that a national cuisine should be. Traditionally, and sensibly, it makes the very best of the seasonal produce from the land and sea and then, in winter, draws nutritiously and deliciously on preserved foods in store. Foods that are produced in abundance – lamb, goat, chicken, fish, certain fruit and vegetables, olive oil and wine – are used in abundance. This might be bad news for some would-be exporters to the country, but it ensures that the traditional cuisine with its unmistakable regional characteristics is handed down, almost unchanged, from one generation to the next.

We are talking mainly, of course, about the cooking you find in Greek homes, whether it is a remote farmhouse way out on a hillside or a tiny fisherman's cottage on the quayside. I would love to say that you could use the recipes in this book as a kind of menu blueprint on your own travels to Greece, but sadly that would be only partly true. It is true that if you seek out unpretentious-looking family-run tavernas way off the tourist track, you will find, to your delight, that the cooking differs little if at all from family fare. Indeed, late in the afternoon after a long and dusty climb we have often collapsed into a tired and hungry heap at the door of a small restaurant and emerged hours later not quite sure whether – apart from the discreet matter of the bill – we had dined as guests of the taverna or the family. A dish of sun-golden courgette flowers deep-fried in the lightest of batters, a heap of spaghetti concealing plump little partridges in a tomato sauce, a casserole of rabbit in red wine, and vine leaves enclosing every imaginable kind of savoury stuffing have come our way with the invitation, 'Well, if you don't mind sharing what we have ourselves.'

But the difference, the uniformity, and the sameness of the food so frequently served in all the old familiar and crowded places – along with their 'international menus' and cups of instant coffee – represents another world entirely – and not a very Greek one at that.

For me, the true cuisine of the country is inextricably bound up with the people I have stayed with and met, whose generosity and hospitality have sometimes been almost overwhelming. On the island of Andros – dare I say it, my favourite of all – three hours or so by boat from Athens, we spent two holidays in a simple farm hut way, way out in the hills and, in exchange for scything fields – my first such experience – and picking olives, shared the best the land could offer – fresh vegetables, cheese and yoghurt made from goat's milk, olive oil pressed from their own fruit, and wine made from their own grapes. No meat. The family didn't have any at that time. There is one wonderful memory I would like to share with you. At the end of each day on the land it was the custom for Adonis, our host, to cut a branch from the pink oleander bushes that flanked the stream and cut a flute from them. Once it was tuned to his satisfaction he shouldered his tools, we did likewise and he piped us off the land and back home, all marching in jaunty step to the traditional and haunting music.

On Siphnos, having expressed my interest in all things culinary, I was invited to collect the family casserole from the bus each morning, lift the lid and sample whatever had been cooked in the baker's oven overnight. Sometimes it would be chick-pea soup, thick and rich and tasty after the long slow cooking, or a dish of goat, tender as lamb after simmering for twelve hours.

By the second day, as soon as he heard on the grapevine that 'friends from abroad' were involved, the baker took to hanging a string bag from the handle of the pot, with a couple of his best cheese pies – still the best I have tasted anywhere in Greece – or custard tarts. And eventually, for good measure, he kindly gave me his special recipes.

On the island of Skyros I wandered up to a group of women sitting knitting on a doorstep and got into conversation about food – the easiest thing in the world to do because the Greeks have no need of our national obsession with the weather. There and then a rota was drawn up: 'You cook that tomorrow, and I'll cook something different the next day.' And for the next two weeks there I was in a different kitchen every morning at seven – before the sun was too hot – helping to make sausages, moussaka – there must be as many diffferent versions as there are cooks in Greece – or chicken pie. And endlessly, as we chopped, stirred and chatted, there would be discussion about such things as how much olive oil to use and the relative merits of using fresh and dried herbs. The general verdict on this weighty subject seemed to be, incidentally, that only oregano is worth using in its dried form.

The generosity and hospitality of the Greek people is legendary, and it was proved to me personally by many an hour sitting whiling away the time under a shady vine, sipping ice-cold water, cups of coffee and tasting sweetmeats and fruit – perhaps my over-riding image of the Greek way of welcome.

What I didn't know until I began collecting material for this book was that the Greeks, unlike some other nations, are as generous with their culinary secrets and family recipes as they are with the food in their cupboards and gardens. And so to everyone who took the time and trouble to measure and list ingredients, show me a particular way of cooking them or invite me to share a family meal – and especially to my Greek teacher, Thorice – I would like to say, sincerely, thank you.

MEZETHES

In a country not blessed with the deep, inky-blue of the Aegean sky, it can sometimes take a vivid imagination to call up those delightful holiday images. Sitting under the welcome shade of a vine or mulberry tree, beside a fishing harbour or even on the edge of a busy street, enjoying a drink before lunch or dinner is one of the great pleasures of Greek life.

Ouzo is the drink to enjoy at times like this. Usually it comes in chubby little glasses, with chilled water to pour on and turn the colourless spirit cloudy.

Mezethes, the whole range of appetizers, are part of the same ritual, and people choose an ouzaria as much for the quality of the little plates of octopus, squid or salads that are served with the drinks as for the atmosphere or the view.

In Greek homes a selection of four or five mezethes will be served, some meat, some fish, some cheese, with crisp slices of fresh vegetables as hors d'oeuvres to enjoy while the conversation flows. Mezethes are meant to be served with pride and appreciated at leisure.

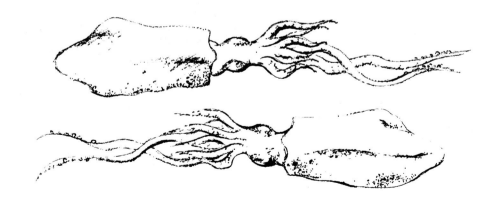

Amigdala Alatismena
Salted Almonds

Makes 1kg/2¼ lb

1kg/2¼ lb shelled but unskinned almonds
50g/2 oz citric acid

150ml/¼ pint water
3 × 15ml/3 tablespoons coarse salt

Place the almonds in a baking dish. Mix the citric acid with the water until it is thoroughly diluted. Pour the liquid over the almonds, shake well and leave for 15 minutes. Strain off all excess liquid.
Sprinkle the salt evenly over the almonds and shake the dish well.
Bake the almonds in the oven at 180°C/350°F/Gas 4 for 30–35 minutes, stirring them frequently. Leave them to cool thoroughly, then store them in a lidded container. They keep in good condition for up to 12 weeks.

Kalamarakia Tiganita
Fried Squid

Serves 4–6

Even people who are not particularly fond of ouzo need little persuading to go to an ouzaria before dinner and order a drink, for the sheer delight of being served with this customary accompaniment.

675g/1½ lb young squid
salt
about 5 × 15ml spoons/5 tablespoons flour

oil for shallow frying
1 lemon, quartered, to serve

Wash the squids thoroughly. Remove the inkbag (this will not be fully formed in the case of very young fish), the head, the entrails and the tentacles. Pull out the transparent backbone. Cut into 6mm/¼ in slices. Wash again and dry well.
Sprinkle the squids with salt and toss them in flour to coat them well. Heat the oil in a heavy based pan and when very hot fry the squid slices a few at a time for 3 minutes, turning them once so that they are evenly brown. Lift them out with a draining spoon and toss on kitchen paper to remove excess fat. Keep them warm while frying the remaining slices in the same way.
Serve the squid hot, with wooden cocktail sticks. Diced cucumber and bread go especially well with them.

Dolmathes
Stuffed Vine Leaves
Makes 24

You will experience a complete sense of well-being when you can enjoy these tiny aromatic parcels with a glass of ouzo under the shade of a vine, but they taste good at home too.

4 × 15ml spoons/4 tablespoons olive oil
2 × 15ml spoons/2 tablespoons pine kernels
1 medium onion, peeled and finely chopped
65g/2½ oz long-grain white rice
150ml/¼ pint water, plus 2 × 15ml spoons/2 tablespoons

salt and freshly ground pepper
2 × 15ml spoons/2 tablespoons currants
40 fresh, canned or bottled vine leaves
1 lemon, quartered, to serve

Heat 1 × 15ml spoon/1 tablespoon of the oil in a pan and fry the pine kernels over moderate heat, stirring frequently, until lightly browned. Remove them with a draining spoon and set aside.

Add 2 × 15ml spoons/2 tablespoons of the remaining oil and fry the onion for 2–3 minutes, stirring frequently, until it is soft and transparent but not beginning to brown. Stir in the rice and cook for 1–2 minutes until well coated with oil. Add 150ml/¼ pint water, salt and pepper, stir well, then cover and simmer over low heat for 12–15 minutes until the rice is tender and has absorbed all the water. Remove from the heat and stir in the pine kernels and currants. Taste, and adjust the seasoning if necessary.

Blanch fresh vine leaves in a large pan of boiling water for 1 minute, rinse, drain and dry. Cover the base of a flameproof casserole with 8 of the leaves and set 8 aside to cover.

Place the remaining 24 leaves, shiny side down, on the work-surface and place about 2 × 5ml spoons/2 teaspoons of the filling in the centre of each. Fold the stalk end over the filling, and roll the parcel over towards the tip of the leaf. Arrange the parcels, join sides down, in the casserole. Sprinkle on the remaining oil and water and cover the parcels with the reserved leaves. Cover the casserole, heat over a moderate flame for 3–4 minutes, then reduce the heat and simmer for 45–50 minutes. Discard the covering layer of vine leaves and set the dish aside to cool.

Serve cold, with lemon wedges.

Melitzano Salata
Aubergine Salad

Serves 4

One of the most delicious ways to enjoy aubergines – puréed, flavoured with onion and garlic and served well chilled.

450g/1 lb 'round' aubergines
1 small onion, peeled and chopped
1 garlic clove, peeled and sliced
1 large ripe tomato, skinned and chopped
4 × 15ml spoons/4 tablespoons olive oil
2 × 5ml spoons/2 teaspoons lemon juice

1 × 5ml spoon/1 teaspoon fresh oregano or
marjoram, if available (do not use dried
herbs)
salt and freshly ground pepper
black olives to garnish

Place the aubergines on a rack in an oven set at 180°C/350°F/Gas 4 and cook, turning them frequently, for 50 minutes, or until they are soft and the skins are black and wrinkled. When they are cool enough to handle, peel off the skins, halve the aubergines, scoop out and discard the seeds and chop the flesh.

Either blend the salad ingredients (aubergines, onion, garlic, tomato, oil, lemon juice and fresh herb if used) in 2 batches or chop the onion more finely, crush the garlic and grind the ingredients to a smooth paste using a pestle and mortar. If blending, process the first batch to a smooth paste, repeat with the second, then mix both together and season with salt and pepper.

Put the salad into a covered container and press a piece of foil onto the surface to prevent a skin from forming. Chill in the refrigerator. The salad will keep in perfect condition for 2–3 days.

Garnish with black olives and serve with fingers of warm pitta bread, thin strips of peppers or 'scoops' of salad leaves.

Taramosalata
Smoked Cod's Roe Salad

Serves 4

175g/6 oz white bread, crusts removed
50g/2 oz salted smoked cod's roe
2 × 15ml spoons/ 2 tablespoons lemon juice
1 small onion, peeled and chopped

100ml/3½ fl oz olive oil or corn oil, or a
mixture
1 × 15ml spoon/1 tablespoon chopped
coriander or parsley, to garnish

This dish was originally made with all the care and attention of a mayonnaise, adding the lemon juice and oil alternately drop by drop. Using a blender cuts down on time with no loss of flavour or texture.
Soak the bread in a bowl of water for 15 minutes, then drain it and squeeze it almost dry. Make the taramosalata in 2 batches, putting half the bread, cod's roe, lemon juice, onion and oil into a blender and processing until smooth and creamy. Repeat with the second batch, then mix both together. Garnish with a few drops of oil, if liked, and with the chopped herb.
Serve with black olives, fingers of warm pitta bread and thin strips of peppers.

Tzatziki
Yoghurt and Cucumber Salad

Serves 4

---

1 × 15ml spoon/1 tablespoon olive oil
1 × 5ml spoon/1 teaspoon lemon juice
1 garlic clove, peeled and crushed
150ml/¼ pint plain yoghurt
10cm/4 in piece cucumber, peeled and finely
chopped

1 × 15ml spoon/1 tablespoon chopped mint
(optional)
salt and freshly ground pepper

Mix the oil and lemon juice and stir in the garlic. Gradually beat in the yoghurt. Stir in the cucumber and mint, if using, and season with salt and pepper.
Serve chilled.

Three of the best-known Greek appetizers:
Taramosalata and Tzatziki (opposite), and Melitzano Salata (page 13)

Tiropitakia
Cheese Triangles
Makes about 24

Once you get into the rhythm of making these little cheese pies, it is easy to make a large batch. If necessary, you can freeze some for another occasion, as they can be reheated perfectly. In this case, double the quantities given.

100g/4 oz ricotta cheese (or use cottage cheese)
150g/6 oz feta cheese (or use Wensleydale)
50g/2 oz kefalotiri or Parmesan cheese, grated
2 small eggs, lightly beaten
2 × 15ml spoons/2 tablespoons chopped parsley

a pinch of grated nutmeg
freshly ground pepper
about 40g/1½ oz butter, melted
225g/8 oz filo pastry
water for sprinkling

Put all the cheeses into a bowl and mash them with a fork. Beat in the eggs and stir in the parsley. Season with nutmeg and pepper.

Brush the bottom of a 23 × 18cm/9 × 7 in metal baking dish with melted butter. Cut the sheets of filo pastry to fit the dish and make a layer of 8 sheets, brushing each one with melted butter. Keep the remaining pastry covered with a damp cloth to prevent it drying out.

Spread the cheese filling over the pastry, then cover it with another 6 sheets of pastry, again brushing each one with melted butter. Brush the top well with butter. Mark the top into triangles, cutting through almost to the cheese filling.

Sprinkle a little water over the pastry top to prevent it from curling at the edges.

Bake the pie in the oven at 190°C/375°F/Gas 5 for 40–45 minutes, until the top is crisp and brown. Cool the pastry slightly and, if it is to be served straight away, cut it into the marked triangles.

If you are handing the pastries round at an indoor drinks party, provide plates or paper napkins – they are delightfully crumbly, but very messy.

Keftedakia
Mini Meat Balls

Makes about 26

Served hot or cold, these tasty little meat balls are ideal as an appetizer to serve at a drinks party.

75g/3 oz white bread, crusts removed, crumbled
2 × 15ml spoons/2 tablespoons ouzo
about 4 × 15ml spoons/4 tablespoons olive oil
1 medium onion, peeled and finely chopped
1 garlic clove, peeled and crushed

450g/1 lb lean minced beef
1 egg, beaten
1 × 15ml spoon/1 tablespoon chopped mint
salt and freshly ground pepper
flour for coating
lemon juice to serve

Put the bread into a large bowl, mash it with a fork, pour on the ouzo and mix well. Leave to blend for 10–15 minutes.

Heat 2 × 15ml spoons/2 tablespoons of the oil in a pan and fry the onion over moderate heat for 3 minutes, stirring once or twice. Add the garlic and cook for 1 minute, until the onions are soft and transparent. Remove the pan from the heat, lift out the onions with a draining spoon and add them to the bread.

Add the minced beef, egg and mint and season with salt and pepper. Beat the mixture well, and either mash it with a wooden spoon until it forms a thick, moist paste or work it in a food processor. Rinse your hands in water and knead the mixture to remove any cracks.

Shape the mixture into balls a little larger than a walnut and roll them in flour to coat them thoroughly. Chill the meatballs for at least 30 minutes.

Heat the remaining oil in the pan and fry the meatballs over moderate heat a few at a time for 7–8 minutes, turning them to brown them evenly. When cooked, remove them with a draining spoon and keep them warm while cooking the remainder in the same way.

Serve the meatballs hot, speared with wooden cocktail sticks, and sprinkled with lemon juice.

Tirakia Tiganita
Cheese Puffs

Makes about 12

2 egg whites
60–75g/2½–3 oz hard cheese such as
  kefalotiri or Parmesan, finely grated

freshly ground pepper
oil for deep frying

Whisk the egg whites until they form stiff peaks. Gradually fold in the cheese
until the mixture is firm enough to shape easily. Season with pepper.
Using a 5ml spoon/teaspoon, form the mixture into small balls about the size
of a walnut and place on a plate, foil or greaseproof paper.
Heat the oil in a deep frying pan until it is 190°C/375°F, or when a cube of
day-old bread will brown in 50 seconds.
Drop the cheese balls into the hot oil a few at a time and fry until they puff up
and turn a light golden brown. Lift them out with a draining spoon and keep
them hot while you fry the remainder.
Serve them as soon as possible, on wooden cocktail sticks.

Tiganito Sikoti
Fried Liver

Serves 8

225g/8 oz calves liver, trimmed and cut into
  2.5cm/1 in cubes
2 × 15ml spoons/2 tablespoons flour
½ × 5ml spoon/½ teaspoon dried thyme
  flowers, or use oregano

40g/1½ oz butter
lemon juice to serve

Mix together the flour and thyme flowers or oregano and toss the liver to
partially coat it.
Heat the butter in a frying pan and when very hot, add the liver and stir it
around with a wooden spoon over moderate heat. Cook for 1½–2 minutes,
until the liver stiffens and becomes golden brown, then lift out, sprinkle with
lemon juice and serve at once. It is specially good served with tomato wedges,
diced cucumber and cubes of bread.

*Cheese Puffs, served with diced cucumber
and black olives*

SOUPS & SAUCES

There's a homeliness and an aura of social history about a pot of soup on the stove. It isn't just a pot of dried beans, fresh vegetables and olive oil; it's a whole culture in a single dish. For soup, real soup, is made from the most plentiful ingredients available, the harvest from the land and sea, and makes no apologies for being simple, unpretentious and good.

I had this brought home to me on the island of Andros once, in a tiny hillside cottage which had an outside cookhouse. After 16 hours on the land our host Adonis brought in a bowl of soup that had been cooking all day. 'Everything I grow is in this pot,' he said simply. 'We will eat, and then we will celebrate. We will dance.' Gratefully, we did.

In much the same way, it seems to me, the sauces that typify Greek home cooking make the most of the food that is there – large, tangy (but never bitter) – lemons for the egg and lemon sauce that flavours everything from soup to a plate of spinach; those huge topsy-turvy tomatoes to serve with macaroni or meat; olive oil – buy the finest unrefined oil you can – to dress fish and fresh vegetables and, that ultimate in flavour sensations, garlic for skorthalia sauce.

Whether it's for soups or sauces, a blend of local ingredients gives you the real flavour of the country.

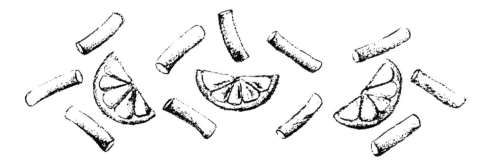

Revythia Soupa
Chick Pea Soup

There's an illusion – quite unfounded – of meat-behind-the-scenes in this country soup.

450g/1 lb dried chick peas, soaked overnight, rinsed and drained
2 litres/3½ pints water
6 × 15ml spoons/6 tablespoons olive oil
2 large onions, peeled and sliced
2 carrots, washed and thinly sliced
2 garlic cloves, peeled and thinly sliced
2 × 15ml spoons/2 tablespoons tomato purée
2 large tomatoes, skinned and sliced
4 × 15ml spoons/4 tablespoons chopped celery leaves
salt and freshly ground pepper
2 × 15ml spoons/2 tablespoons lemon juice
4 × 15ml spoons/4 tablespoons chopped parsley

Put the chick peas in a pan, cover with water and bring to the boil. Fast-boil, covered, for 15 minutes, then drain, discarding the liquid.

Return the chick peas to the pan, pour on 2 litres/3½ pints water and bring to the boil. Skim off any foam that rises to the surface. Cover the pan and simmer for 1¾ hours, or until the chick peas are tender.

Meanwhile, heat the oil in a pan. Sauté the onions, carrots and garlic over moderate heat for 5–6 minutes, stirring frequently, until they begin to turn brown. Stir in the tomato purée and sliced tomatoes and cook for 5 minutes. Remove about 4 × 15ml spoons/4 tablespoons of the chick peas with a draining spoon and set aside. Stir the vegetable mixture into the chick peas in the pan.

Purée the soup in a blender, then return it to the pan and add the reserved chick peas. Season with salt and pepper, stir in the lemon juice and reheat gently. Serve garnished with the parsley.

Fassoulatha
Haricot Bean Soup

Serves 4

Tomatoes, olive oil and dried beans – the proud harvest of many a country family – combine in a soup I was first offered in a humble cottage on Andros. After I had helped to scythe a field of vetch!

225g/8 oz dried haricot beans, soaked overnight and drained
150ml/¼ pint olive oil
2 large onions, peeled and sliced
2 garlic cloves, peeled and chopped
450g/1 lb tomatoes, skinned and sliced, or use 1 × 400g/14 oz can

1 × 5ml spoon/1 teaspoon tomato purée
1 bay leaf
½ × 5ml spoon/½ teaspoon dried oregano
450ml/¾ pint water
salt and freshly ground pepper
1 × 15ml spoon/1 tablespoon chopped parsley

Put the beans in a large pan, cover with cold water and bring to the boil. Cover the pan and fast-boil for 15 minutes. Drain the beans into a colander. Heat the oil in the same pan and fry the onions and garlic over moderate heat for 5 minutes. Add the beans and cook in the oil for a further 3 minutes. Add the tomatoes, tomato purée, bay leaf, oregano and water and stir well. Season with pepper.
Bring to the boil, cover and simmer over low heat for 1 hour, or until the beans are tender. Season, then taste and adjust seasoning if necessary.
Sprinkle with the parsley to garnish.

Haricot Bean Soup

Soupa Avgolemono
Egg and Lemon Soup

Serves 4

There's very little to this soup – it all depends on the homely quality of the stock, the kind that used to simmer on the stove for hours.

1 litre/1¾ pints well-flavoured home-made chicken stock
75g/3 oz short-grain rice, washed and drained
3 eggs, separated

4 × 15ml spoons/4 tablespoons lemon juice
salt and freshly ground pepper
2 × 15ml spoons/2 tablespoons chopped coriander or parsley
4 thin slices lemon to serve

Bring the stock to the boil, add the rice, stir and return to the boil. Cover the pan and boil gently for 15 minutes, until the rice is tender. Skim off any fat that has risen to the surface. Allow to cool slightly.

Whisk the egg whites until stiff, then beat in the yolks. Gradually beat in the lemon juice. Stir in about 150ml/¼ pint of the hot soup – do not add it while at boiling point or the eggs will scramble – and beat thoroughly.

Add the egg mixture to the soup and heat gently, taking care not to let it boil. Season with salt and pepper and set aside for about 3 minutes for the flavours to blend.

Sprinkle with the chopped herb to garnish and serve a slice of lemon with each portion.

Note Add about 150g/6 oz chopped cooked chicken for extra flavour if you wish.

Soupa Faki
Lentil Soup

Serves 4–6

350g/12 oz brown continental lentils, washed
   and drained
1 litre/1¾ pints water
1 large onion, peeled and sliced
2 garlic cloves, peeled and thinly sliced
4 stalks tender celery, thinly sliced
2 carrots, thinly sliced
150ml/¼ pint olive oil

350g/12 oz tomatoes, skinned and sliced
1 × 15ml spoon/1 tablespoon tomato purée
4–5 stalks fresh thyme or parsley
salt and freshly ground pepper
2 × 15ml spoons/2 tablespoons white wine
   vinegar
1 × 15ml spoon/1 tablespoon chopped thyme
   or parsley to serve

Put the lentils into a large pan, cover with water and bring to the boil. Boil for
5 minutes. Strain the lentils into a colander and discard the liquid.
Return the lentils to the pan, pour on 1 litre/1¾ pints water and add the
onion, garlic, celery, carrots, oil, tomatoes and tomato purée. Stir well, add
the herb stalks and bring to the boil. Cover and simmer for 45 minutes,
adding a little more water if necessary. Discard the herb stalks.
Season the soup with salt and pepper and stir in the vinegar. Set the soup
aside for 2–3 minutes before serving sprinkled with the chopped herb.

Kalamarasoupa Me Domata
Squid and Tomato Soup

Serves 4

450g/1 lb squids
150ml/¼ pint olive oil
1 large onion, peeled and sliced
2 garlic cloves, peeled and thinly sliced
350g/12 oz tomatoes, skinned and sliced
150ml/¼ pint red wine

100g/4 oz mushrooms, sliced
600ml/1 pint water
freshly ground pepper
3 × 15ml spoons/3 tablespoons chopped
   parsley

Clean the squids as described on page 11. Cut them into 4cm/1½ in slices.
Heat the oil in a pan and fry the onions and garlic over moderate heat for 4
minutes. Add the squids, tomatoes, wine, mushrooms and water and bring
slowly to the boil. Cover and simmer for 10 minutes.
Season with pepper, then stir in most of the parsley, reserving a
little to garnish.

Psarosoupa
Fish Soup
Serves 4–6

It's hard to believe that something so tasty can be prepared on a fishing boat at sea; it must have something to do with the freshness of the fish! The soup is colloquially named after the earthenware pot in which it is cooked, kakavia.

1.4kg/3 lb white fish on the bone or a mixture of fish
2 large onions, peeled and sliced
4 stalks celery, sliced
4 carrots, sliced
2 bay leaves
2 litres/3½ pints water
3 × 15ml spoons/3 tablespoons olive oil

2 garlic cloves, peeled and crushed
4 large tomatoes, skinned and chopped
4 medium potatoes, peeled and sliced
100ml/3½ fl oz dry white wine
salt and freshly ground pepper
2 × 15ml spoons/2 tablespoons lemon juice
2 × 15ml spoons/2 tablespoons chopped parsley

Trim the fish and remove the bones. Wash the fish, cut it into 7.5cm/3 in slices and set aside.

Put the fish trimmings into a pan with half the onion, celery, carrots and 1 bay leaf. Pour on the water, bring to the boil, cover and simmer for 45 minutes. Strain the stock.

Heat the oil in the pan and add the remaining onion, celery, carrots and bay leaf, the garlic, tomatoes and potato. Bring to the boil, cover the pan and simmer for 30 minutes.

Pour on the wine, season with salt and pepper and add the fish. Simmer for 10 minutes. Stir in the lemon juice and simmer for 3–4 minutes. Taste the soup and adjust the seasoning if necessary. Discard the bay leaf. Serve garnished with the parsley.

Fish Soup, traditionally cooked in an earthenware pot

Saltsa Avgolemono
Egg and Lemon Sauce

Makes about 200ml/7 fl oz

2 eggs
1 × 15ml spoon/1 tablespoon water
4–5 × 15ml spoons/4–5 tablespoons lemon
   juice

4 × 15ml spoons/4 tablespoons hot stock from
   a soup or casserole (see below)

Beat the eggs with the water until well mixed, then beat in the lemon juice. Gradually beat in hot, but not boiling stock. If the egg and lemon sauce is to be stirred into a soup or casserole, you then whisk the sauce into the dish and heat it very gently, without boiling. If the sauce is to serve with another dish, use a light chicken or vegetable stock, then pour the mixture into the top of a double boiler, or into a bowl over a pan of simmering water, and whisk until it thickens. Do not let the water touch the container, or the eggs in the sauce will scramble. There is always a danger of this and, though simple to make, the sauce does need undivided attention for a few minutes.

Skorthalia
Garlic Sauce

Serves 8

The last time I was staying in Greece a friend got so hooked on skorthalia that he asked for it with everything – beans, roast lamb, grilled fish and, with chunks of bread, as a meze. Use more or less garlic according to your taste.

225g/8 oz stale bread, crusts removed,
   crumbled
4 garlic cloves, peeled and sliced

1 × 15ml spoon/1 tablespoon wine vinegar
6 × 15ml spoons/6 tablespoons olive oil
freshly ground pepper

Soak the bread in water for 15 minutes, then press out the excess moisture. Put the bread, garlic, vinegar and oil in a blender and process to make a smooth paste. Alternatively grind the ingredients thoroughly using a pestle and mortar. Add a very little water if the paste is too dry, and season with a grind of pepper.
Store in a lidded container. The sauce will keep well for several days.
Use it sparingly, as a dip or a side sauce.

Saltsa Domata
Tomato Sauce

Makes about 750ml/1¼ pints

50g/2 oz butter or 5 × 15ml spoons/5
  tablespoons olive oil
1 large onion, peeled and finely chopped
2 garlic cloves, peeled and finely chopped
1 kg/2¼ lb tomatoes, skinned, or 2 × 400g/
  14 oz cans
1 bay leaf
1 × 5ml spoon/1 teaspoon fresh basil or ½ ×
  5ml spoon/½ teaspoon dried oregano

1 × 5ml spoon/1 teaspoon sugar
a pinch of cinnamon
1 × 5ml spoon/1 teaspoon tomato purée
100ml/3½ fl oz red wine (or use more water)
150ml/¼ pint water (only if fresh tomatoes
  are used)
salt and freshly ground pepper

Heat the butter or oil and fry the onion and garlic over moderate heat for 3–4
minutes, stirring once or twice. Add the tomatoes, bay leaf, herb, sugar,
cinnamon and tomato purée, stir well and bring to the boil. Simmer
for 15 minutes.
Pour on the wine, if using, and the water and season with salt and pepper.
Bring the sauce to the boil and simmer, uncovered, for 30 minutes. Discard
the bay leaf, taste the sauce and adjust the seasoning if necessary.
If the sauce is a little too liquid, increase the heat to reduce it slightly.

Latholemono
Oil and Lemon Dressing

Makes about 150ml/¼ pint

150ml/¼ pint olive oil
3 × 15ml spoons/3 tablespoons lemon juice
2 × 15ml spoons/2 tablespoons chopped
  parsley or marjoram

salt and freshly ground pepper
a pinch of sugar (optional)

Put all the ingredients into a screw-top jar and shake well. Store the sauce at
room temperature and shake it well before you use it.
The sauce is best made a few hours in advance, so that the flavours can blend.

FISH

Coastal Greece presents a series of images – of the colourful fishing boats bob-bobbing in the benign waters of the harbours or being battered about by the hostile elements that can strike so unexpectedly and suddenly. I even have – and I think this is rare – a lasting memory of an anxious inter-island trip in a caique steered by a swarthy Naxos *psaras* protecting himself from the storm with a huge black 'city' umbrella.

Then there are the quay-side fish markets, treasure-troves of glinting, glistening, shining fish of every size and shape, such variety it seems you could enjoy a different species, prepared in a different way, for every meal in a year.

Away from Greece, we sadly have less choice, and there are fewer and fewer shops offering a really delectable selection of fresh fish. For this reason, many of the recipes that follow are deliberately non-specific about the type of fish, and any 'white fish steaks' or 'oily fish' can be substituted. What we can borrow from the country to make the dishes distinctly Greek are the characteristic flavour combinations, of good olive oil, tomatoes, herbs, lemons and olives, and the many ways of preparing and cooking them.

Greek fish cookery can include simmering, baking, grilling, frying or stewing; but the important aspect of it is making the very best of the sea harvest.

Rizi Pilafi me Mithia
Mussel Pilaff

Serves 4

In an ideal world – on the islands – you wander along the beach, collect your mussels and go and have a drink in the taverna while they cook the pilaff for you.

1 litre/2¼ pints mussels
100ml/3½ fl oz olive oil
2 medium onions, peeled and finely chopped
1 litre/1¾ pints water
100ml/3½ fl oz white wine

350g/12 oz long-grain rice
salt and freshly ground pepper
3 × 15ml spoons/3 tablespoons chopped
   parsley

Thoroughly wash the mussels in several buckets of water and scrub off the black 'beards'. Discard any mussels that have opened.

Heat the oil in a large pan and fry the onion over moderate heat for 3–4 minutes, stirring once or twice. Add the mussels and stir with a wooden spoon until the shells open. Pour on the water and wine and bring to the boil. Simmer for 10 minutes.

Lift out the mussels with a draining spoon and discard any whose shells have not opened (a reverse of the earlier quality control).

Stir the rice into the mussel liquor and season with salt and pepper. Cover and cook for 10–12 minutes, until just tender.

Meanwhile, remove the mussels from the shells, then stir them into the rice.

Cover the pan and leave it on the side of the stove for 5 minutes, for the flavours to blend. Sprinkle with the parsley.

Mithia Tiganita
Deep-fried Mussels

Serves 4

1 litre/2¼ pints mussels
oil for deep frying
1 lemon, quartered, to serve
skorthalia (see page 00), to serve
BATTER:
2 eggs

50g/2 oz flour
4 × 15ml spoons/4 tablespoons water
salt and freshly ground pepper
2 × 15ml spoons/2 tablespoons chopped
  parsley
a pinch of ground cinnamon

Wash, clean and cook the mussels as described in the previous recipe. Drain
them and take them out of their shells. The liquor can be reserved for
a fish soup.
To make the batter, beat the eggs, gradually beat in the flour and then the
water. Season with salt and pepper and stir in the parsley and cinnamon.
Heat the oil for deep frying to a temperature of 180°C/350°F, or when a cube
of day-old bread will brown in 60 seconds.
Dip the mussels in the batter, drain off any excess and fry them a few at a time
in the hot oil. Drain them on kitchen paper and keep them warm while you
fry the remainder.
Serve the mussels hot, with wedges of lemon.

Sardeles sto Fourno
Baked Sardines

Serves 4

1kg/2¼ lb fresh sardines, cleaned, gutted,
  washed and drained
salt and freshly ground pepper
200ml/7 fl oz olive oil

10 × 15ml spoons/10 tablespoons lemon juice
3 × 15ml spoons/3 tablespoons chopped
  marjoram

Season the fish with salt and pepper. Mix together the oil and lemon juice, stir
in 2 × 15ml spoons/2 tablespoons of the marjoram and season with
salt and pepper.
Arrange the fish in a shallow baking dish and pour the dressing over.
Bake in the oven at 190°C/375°F/Gas 5 for 15 minutes. Sprinkle with the
remaining herb and serve at once.

Astakos me Latholemono
Lobster with Oil and Lemon Dressing

Serves 2

1 spiny lobster, about 900g/2 lb
150ml/¼ pint olive oil
3 × 15ml spoons/3 tablespoons lemon juice

1 × 15ml spoon/1 tablespoon chopped
  marjoram or parsley
salt and freshly ground pepper

If you buy a live lobster, plunge it into a large pan of fast-boiling water for 1 minute, then into cold water. Drain and split the lobster in half lengthways. Discard the entrails, wash the lobster under cold running water and drain again. Scrape out the flesh from the body and tail and slice it.
Mix together the oil, lemon juice and herb and season the dressing with salt and pepper.
Stir the lobster into the dressing and pile it back into the two half-shells. Place the lobster halves, shell side up, on a grill rack and grill under moderate heat for 5 minutes. Turn the shells, brush the flesh with the remaining dressing and grill for 7–8 minutes. Serve at once.

Garithes me Feta
Prawns in Wine and Cheese Sauce

Serves 4

4 × 15ml spoons/4 tablespoons olive oil
4 spring onions, peeled and finely chopped
2 garlic cloves, peeled and finely chopped
450g/1 lb tomatoes, skinned, seeded and
  chopped
100ml/3½ fl oz white wine
1 × 5ml spoon/1 teaspoon sugar

3 × 15ml spoons/ 3 tablespoons chopped
  parsley
salt and freshly ground pepper
675g/1½ lb large raw prawns, washed and
  drained
100g/4 oz feta cheese, crumbled (or use
  ricotta)

Heat the oil in a frying-pan and fry the onions over moderate heat for 4–5 minutes, stirring once or twice. Add the garlic, tomatoes, wine, sugar and parsley and season with salt and pepper. Bring to the boil and simmer for 15–20 minutes, until the sauce thickens.
Add the prawns and simmer for 7–8 minutes. Stir in the cheese and cook for 2–3 minutes, until it just begins to melt.
Serve at once. The prawns are peeled at the table and eaten with the fingers.

Rizi Pilafi me Garithes
Prawn Pilaff

Serves 4

This is just the kind of light lunch dish, somewhere between mezethes and a 'proper meal', to enjoy on the balcony with a glass of dry white wine.

3 × 15ml spoons/3 tablespoons olive oil
1 medium onion, peeled and sliced
2 garlic cloves, peeled and finely chopped
100g/4 oz long-grain rice
350g/12 oz tomatoes, skinned and chopped
2 × 15ml spoons/2 tablespoons chopped
    marjoram or 2 × 5ml spoons/2 teaspoons
    dried oregano
salt and freshly ground pepper

150ml/¼ pint water
1 × 5ml spoon/1 teaspoon sugar
1 × 5ml spoon/1 teaspoon lemon juice
350g/12 oz cooked and shelled prawns
100g/4 oz feta cheese, crumbled (or use
    Wensleydale)
2 × 15ml spoons/2 tablespoons chopped
    parsley

Heat the oil in a frying-pan and fry the onion and garlic over moderate heat for 3–4 minutes, stirring once or twice. Stir in the rice and cook for 1 minute. Stir in the tomatoes and herb and season with salt and pepper. Pour on the water, add the sugar and lemon juice and bring to the boil.
Cover the pan and simmer over low heat for 10 minutes. Stir in the peeled prawns and cook for 5 minutes more, or until the rice is just tender.
Stir in the cheese and set the pan aside for 2–3 minutes, until the cheese begins to melt.
Serve the pilaff garnished with the parsley.

Prawn Pilaff

Psari Spetsiotiko
Baked Fish, Spetsai Style

Serves 6

There is a wide and confusing variety of fish available in Greece, each one with its own special flavour. Whichever you can buy, it will be subtle and delicate cooked as they do on the island of Spetsai.

150ml/¼ pint olive oil
1 whole fish such as bream, about 1kg/2¼ lb,
    cleaned and gutted
3 × 15ml spoons/3 tablespoons lemon juice
salt and freshly ground pepper
3 thin slices lemon
4 × 15ml spoons/4 tablespoons chopped
    mixed herbs, such as basil, marjoram and
    parsley

2 garlic cloves, peeled and finely chopped
100ml/3½ fl oz white wine
350g/12 oz tomatoes, skinned and chopped
1 × 15ml spoon/1 tablespoon tomato purée
75g/3oz dry white breadcrumbs

Brush a roasting pan with a little of the oil. Sprinkle the fish inside and out with lemon juice and season it with salt and pepper. Place the lemon slices and 2 × 15ml spoons/2 tablespoons of the herbs inside the fish and put the fish in the pan.

Mix together the remaining oil, garlic, wine, tomatoes and tomato purée and season with salt and pepper. Pour the sauce over the fish and sprinkle on half the breadcrumbs.

Bake the fish, uncovered, in the oven at 190°C/375°F/Gas 5 for 20 minutes. Turn the fish over carefully, using 2 fish slices. Spoon the sauce over to cover the fish and sprinkle on the remaining crumbs. Bake for a further 20–25 minutes, until the fish is tender.

Serve with salad.

Psari Yiahni Me Lahano
Fish and Vegetable Casserole
Serves 4

One of those delightful all-in-together recipes that takes no time at all to prepare, and leaves the cook free to enjoy a glass of ouzo.

1kg/2¼ lb piece of fish, such as codling
1.5 litres/2½ pints water
150ml/¼ pint olive oil
350g/12 oz pickling-sized onions, peeled but whole
4 medium carrots, halved lengthways
8 small courgettes, trimmed
350g/12 oz small potatoes, scrubbed and sliced

1 small root celeriac, scrubbed and thinly sliced
1 bunch of parsley stalks
salt and freshly ground pepper
SAUCE:
2 eggs
4 × 15ml spoons/4 tablespoons lemon juice
salt and freshly ground pepper

Put the fish in a fish kettle or roasting pan, pour on the water and oil, add all the vegetables and parsley and season with salt and pepper. Bring to the boil, cover and simmer for 10–15 minutes, until the fish is just tender.
Lift the fish out on to a serving dish. Drain the vegetables and arrange them around it. Cover with foil and keep warm.
Beat the eggs and beat in the lemon juice. Gradually pour on 6 × 15ml spoons/6 tablespoons of the fish liquor and season with salt and pepper. Heat very gently for 1–2 minutes, but on no account allow the sauce to boil.
Pour the sauce over the fish and serve at once.

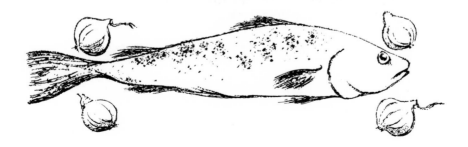

Barbounia se Lethoharto
Baked Red Mullet

Serves 4

Red mullet is *the* fish of Greece, from Kalymnos to Kea. And very expensive always.
When you can buy it in the UK it's somewhat cheaper, so it's worth buying
some to freeze.

4 red mullet, about 300g/10 oz each, cleaned
about 8 × 15ml spoons/8 tablespoons olive oil
4 × 15ml spoons/4 tablespoons lemon juice

salt and freshly ground pepper
2 × 15ml spoons/2 tablespoons chopped
  thyme or parsley
1 lemon, thinly sliced

Brush the fish with 2 × 15ml spoons/2 tablespoons of the oil.
Cut 4 pieces of foil or greasproof paper about 30cm/12 in square and brush
the centres with oil.
Mix together 4 × 15ml spoons/4 tablespoons each of oil and lemon juice.
Season with salt and pepper and stir in the herb.
Slightly gather up the sides of the foil or paper squares to make a dish shape.
Pour the dressing over the fish and divide the lemon slices between them.
Fold over to enclose the fish and make neat, leakproof parcels and brush
these with oil to prevent them burning.
Place the parcels on a baking tray and cook them in the oven at 190°C/375°F/
Gas 5 for 25 minutes, or until the fish is cooked.
Serve with salad.

Baked Red Mullet with a country-style salad

Psari Tiganito me Meli
Pan-fried Fish with Honey

Serves 4

'I'll cook you a dish that will make you dream of Greece for ever,' promised our host on Evia. With thin steaks of sviritha, an expensive and succulent fish, he created a simple masterpiece.

4 halibut steaks, or similar
4 × 15ml spoons/4 tablespoons flour
salt and freshly ground pepper
2 × 15ml spoons/2 tablespoons dried oregano
4 × 15ml spoons/4 tablespoons olive oil
25g/1 oz butter
1 medium onion, peeled and finely chopped

150ml/¼ pint water
2 × 15ml spoons/2 tablespoons clear honey
½ × 5ml spoon/½ teaspoon made mustard
SAUCE:
2 egg yolks
3 × 15ml spoons/3 tablespoons lemon juice

Wipe the fish steaks with a damp cloth and dry them well. Toss them in flour seasoned with salt, pepper and oregano.

Heat the oil and butter in a large pan and when very hot add the fish. Fry quickly over high heat for 2–3 minutes on each side, then lift out the fish and reduce the heat to moderate.

Add the onion and fry for 3–4 minutes, stirring once or twice. Pour on the water, stir in the honey and mustard, season with salt and pepper and bring to the boil. Simmer for 5 minutes.

To make the sauce, beat the egg yolks, beat in the lemon juice and then 4–5 × 15ml spoons/4–5 tablespoons of the liquor from the pan. Pour the egg mixture into the pan, stir well, add the fish and reduce the heat to low.

Simmer very gently for 2–3 minutes, but do not allow the sauce to boil.

Psari sta Klimatofilla
Grilled Fish in Vine Leaves

Serves 4

Vine leaves make the most perfect 'envelopes', and are especially good with oily fish. Here's a good way to prepare fish to cook on a barbecue.

4 small mackerel or herring, cleaned and gutted
3 × 15ml spoons/3 tablespoons lemon juice
salt and freshly ground pepper
a little olive oil
2 × 15ml spoons/2 tablespoons chopped thyme

8–12 sprigs fresh thyme, if available
about 12 fresh young vine leaves, or bottled ones, rinsed, drained and dried
150ml/¼ pint oil and lemon dressing (see page 29)
2 lemons, halved, to serve

Scrape the scales from the fish, wash and dry them. Sprinkle the fish inside and out with the lemon juice and season them with salt and pepper. Brush the fish well with oil – this will have the effect of brushing in the seasoning. Sprinkle the fish with the thyme and, if you have them, place sprigs of thyme in the cavities.

Brush the vine leaves on both sides with oil and wrap the fish in them to enclose them completely.

Grill the fish under moderate heat for 5–6 minutes on each side, brushing the vine leaves frequently with oil.

Serve with the lemon wedges.

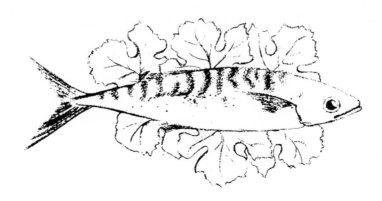

Ochtapothi Stifado
Simmered Octopus

Serves 4–6

I remember once, on Paros, being invited (in sign language) to lift the lid of a deep pot resting over a charcoal fire, right down by Naoussa harbour. And this is what I found.

1kg/2¼ lb young octopus
150ml/¼ pint olive oil
450g/1 lb onions, peeled and sliced
4 garlic cloves, peeled and finely chopped
100ml/3½ fl oz white wine vinegar
100ml/3½ fl oz white wine

4 × 15ml spoons/4 tablespoons tomato purée
350g/12 oz potatoes, peeled and sliced
salt and freshly ground pepper
4 × 15ml spoons/4 tablespoons chopped
* parsley*

Clean the octopus as described on page 11 and remove the ink-bag. Cut off the tentacles and slice the body.

Heat the oil and cook the onions over moderate heat for 5 minutes.

Add the garlic and octopus and simmer for a further 5 minutes. Add the vinegar, wine and tomato purée and stir well until the sauce is thoroughly blended.

Cover the pan and simmer for 2 hours.

Add the potatoes, season with salt and pepper and stir in half the parsley. Bring to the boil and simmer for 30 minutes, until the octopus and potatoes are tender. Taste the sauce and adjust the seasoning if necessary.

Sprinkle with the remaining parsley.

MEAT

Lamb and pork sizzling on a spit; chops and steak browning over a charcoal grid; beef or chicken simmering in a casserole with tomatoes and spices; a whole rabbit in a roasting pan, sometimes sent to be cooked at the baker's; lamb chops and cheese wrapped protectively in greasproof paper parcels to seal in all the flavour – however it is cooked, meat from the mountains or the pastures is enticingly full of the aroma of wild herbs.

Meat is never taken for granted in Greece – an attitude which goes back to the days when religious fasting was observed more rigorously, and when many families could afford such a luxury only once or twice a week in any case. So every dish is considered somewhat special, and prepared with care.

Lamb is far and away the favourite, cooked whole for the celebration of Easter and in simpler ways on lesser days. In many of the regions goat is a speciality, similar in texture to mutton, but with a stronger flavour. If you can obtain it, substitute it for lamb in these recipes; it will take longer to cook and become tender, but you will experience one of the most memorable flavours Greece has to offer.

In a shop by the beach in Siphnos our hostess sent for a take-away across the road – a casserole of goat with celeriac and pasta. And on Samos, before I fully understood the mysteries of metrication, I ordered two kilos of spit-roast leg of goat for the two of us, instead of two pounds. I have to admit – it was too good to waste.

Arni Palikari
Lamb Chops with Cheese

Serves 4

The unusual combination of lamb and cheese, cooked in parcels, 'bandit style', makes a very rich dish which is especially good with a simple green salad.

4 chump chops of lamb
25g/1 oz butter
1 large onion, peeled and sliced
2 garlic cloves, peeled and chopped
4 medium tomatoes, sliced

2 × 5ml spoons/2 teaspoons dried oregano
salt and freshly ground pepper
2 medium potatoes, peeled and sliced
75g/3 oz kaseri or Gruyère cheese, thinly sliced

Fry the chops with no extra fat in a frying pan over moderate heat for 3 minutes on each side. Lift them out and place each one in the centre of a 30cm/12 in square of foil or greaseproof paper – the latter is more authentic. Wipe the pan dry with kitchen paper, melt the butter and fry the onion and garlic for 3–4 minutes, stirring once or twice. Lift out the onion with a draining spoon and scatter it over the meat. Arrange the tomato slices on top and sprinkle with the oregano. Season with salt and pepper. Arrange the potato slices over the tomatoes and cover with the cheese.

Fold the foil or greaseproof paper to make leak-proof parcels. Brush the paper parcels with oil, place them on a baking tray and cook them in the oven at 180°C/350°F/Gas 4 for 1½–1¾ hours. The potatoes should be very soft and the cheese melted and gooey. Serve in the paper to preserve both the flavour and the element of surprise.

Souvlakia
Lamb Kebabs

Serves 4

Small skewers of lamb are part of the Greek way of life. The bus rumbling across the island of Crete stops at a roadside charcoal burner and everyone piles out to buy them; they are served as a first course, part of a main course or just as a snack. The secret of that special flavour is the lemon.

3 × 15ml spoons/3 tablespoons olive oil
3 × 15ml spoons/3 tablespoons lemon juice
2 × 15ml spoons/2 tablespoons fresh thyme or 2 × 5ml spoons/2 teaspoons dried oregano
1 garlic clove, peeled and crushed
freshly ground pepper

1kg/2¼ lb lean lamb, cut into 4cm/1½ in cubes
2 bay leaves, crumbled, plus 4 whole bay leaves
1 lemon, quartered, to serve

Make the marinade by beating together the oil, lemon juice, herb and garlic, and season with pepper. Place the meat and crumbled bay leaves in a plastic bag, pour in the marinade, seal the bag and turn it over and over. Leave in a cool place for about 2 hours, turning the bag once if it is convenient.

Lift out the lamb with a draining spoon and pour any remaining marinade into a bowl. Thread a bay leaf on to each of 4 skewers and divide the cubes of lamb between them.

Cook the kebabs under a hot grill for about 5 minutes, turning them frequently and brushing with the remaining marinade.

Serve with a wedge of lemon and warm pitta bread.

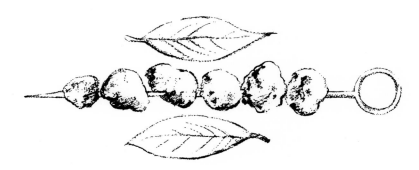

Arni Yiouvetsi
Roast Leg of Lamb with Pasta

Serves 4–6

All the flavour of the meat and the garlic is there in the pasta surrounding it, a perfect combination. The addition of carrots, a departure from the traditional recipe, comes from a friend on Evia.

1.5–1.75kg/3½–4 lb leg of lamb, trimmed of excess fat
2 garlic cloves, peeled and thinly sliced
2 × 15ml spoons/2 tablespoons lemon juice
1 × 5ml spoon/1 teaspoon dried oregano
salt and freshly ground pepper
1 large onion, peeled and roughly chopped

2 medium carrots
6 × 15ml spoons/6 tablespoons water
225g/8 oz orzo (rice-like pasta)
2 × 15ml spoons/ 2 tablespoons tomato purée
2 × 15ml spoons/2 tablespoons kefalotiri or Parmesan cheese, grated

Make slits in the lamb and press in the slivers of garlic. Rub the lemon juice well into the meat. Sprinkle the meat with oregano, salt and pepper, rubbing the seasoning well in.

Place the lamb on a rack in a roasting pan and cook in the oven at 220°C/425°F/Gas 7 for 15 minutes. Reduce the heat to 180°C/350°F/Gas 4. Arrange the onion and carrot slices around the meat and sprinkle the water over them. Roast for a further 40–50 minutes, until the meat is cooked to your liking.

Cook the pasta in a large pan of boiling, salted water for 10 minutes, or until just tender. Drain it into a colander and refresh it by running hot water through it. Drain.

Transfer the lamb to a heated serving dish and set aside to keep warm. Skim off the fat from the roasting pan and stir in the tomato purée and pasta. Season with salt and pepper and return the pan to the oven for 10 minutes.

Arrange the pasta around the meat and sprinkle it with the cheese.

Roast Leg of Lamb with Pasta

Pastitsio
Lamb and Macaroni Casserole

Serves 6

225g/8 oz ziti (elbow macaroni), washed and drained
salt and freshly ground pepper
2 × 15ml spoons/2 tablespoons oil
1 large onion, peeled and finely chopped
450g/1 lb lean minced lamb
3 large tomatoes, skinned, seeded and sliced
3 × 15ml spoons/3 tablespoons tomato purée
2 garlic cloves, peeled and crushed
1 × 5ml spoon/1 teaspoon dried oregano

50g/2 oz kefalotiri or Parmesan cheese, grated
3 × 15ml spoons/3 tablespoons breadcrumbs
SAUCE:
25g/1 oz butter
25g/1 oz flour
450ml/¾ pint milk
salt and freshly ground pepper
a pinch of ground cinnamon
3 eggs

Cook the pasta in a large, covered pan of boiling, salted water for about 12 minutes, or until it is just tender. Drain it into a colander and refresh it by running hot water through it.

Heat the oil in a pan and fry the onion over moderate heat for 3 minutes, stirring once or twice. Add the lamb and stir well. Cook for 5 minutes, stirring frequently, so that it is evenly browned.

Add the tomatoes, tomato purée, garlic and oregano and season with salt and pepper. Bring to the boil, cover the pan and simmer for 15 minutes.

To make the egg sauce, melt the butter and stir in the flour. When it has formed a thick paste, gradually pour on the milk, stirring constantly. Bring to the boil and simmer for 2 minutes. Remove from the heat, season the sauce with salt, pepper and cinnamon and beat in the eggs.

To assemble the dish, spread half the pasta into a greased, shallow baking dish. Cover it with half the meat, then half the egg sauce and half the cheese. Repeat the layers in the same order, mixing the breadcrumbs with the cheese for the topping.

Pre-heat the oven to 190°C/375°F/Gas 5, place the dish on a baking tray, and bake for 40 minutes, until the top is deep golden brown and bubbling.

Serve hot, warm or cold, depending on just how Greek you want to be!

Arni se Lethoharto
Marinated Lamb Parcels

Serves 4

1.1kg/2½ lb boned leg of lamb, trimmed of
    fat and cut into 7.5–10cm/3–4 in slices
4 garlic cloves, peeled and thinly sliced
4 × 15ml spoons/4 tablespoons olive oil
4 × 15ml spoons/4 tablespoons red wine

salt and freshly ground pepper
2 × 15ml spoons/2 tablespoons fresh
    marjoram or 2 × 5ml spoons/2 teaspoons
    dried oregano

Dry the meat. Cut slits in it and insert the slivers of garlic. Mix together the oil, wine, salt and pepper and toss the meat in the mixture.
Brush 4 × 30cm/12 in squares of foil or greaseproof paper with oil and place the meat and marinade in the centre of each. Sprinkle with the herb and fold over the wrapping to make leak-proof parcels. Brush the paper parcels with oil and place them close together in a shallow baking dish. Cook in the oven at 170°C/325°F/Gas 3 for 3 hours. Serve the parcels still wrapped.

Kouneli Lemonato
Rabbit in Lemon Sauce

Serves 4

---

1 rabbit, jointed
3 × 15ml spoons/3 tablespoons vinegar
salt and freshly ground pepper
100ml/3½ fl oz olive oil
25g/1 oz butter

4 × 15ml spoons/4 tablespoons lemon juice
300ml/½ pint hot chicken stock
1 × 15ml spoon/1 tablespoon chopped basil or
    1 × 5ml spoon/1 teaspoon dried oregano

Soak the rabbit overnight in a bowl of water with the vinegar.
Drain and dry the rabbit and season it well with salt and pepper. Heat the oil and butter in a pan and fry the rabbit pieces for 10 minutes, turning frequently. Pour on the lemon juice and stock, season with salt and pepper and add the herb. Bring the sauce to the boil, cover the pan and simmer slowly for 1¼ hours, or until the meat is tender.
Transfer the meat to a heated serving dish. Boil the sauce to reduce it slightly and adjust the seasoning if needed.

Moussaka
Lamb and Aubergine Pie
Serves 6

1kg/2¼ lb aubergines, cut into 1cm/½ inch slices
salt and freshly ground pepper
about 50g/2 oz flour for coating
about 300ml/½ pint olive oil
2 medium onions, peeled and sliced
450g/1 lb lean minced lamb
4 medium tomatoes, skinned and sliced, or 1 × 400g/14 oz can tomatoes, drained
3 × 15ml spoons/3 tablespoons tomato purée
2 garlic cloves, peeled and finely chopped

2 × 5ml spoons/2 teaspoons dried oregano
a pinch of ground cinnamon
SAUCE:
15g/½ oz butter
25g/1 oz flour
300ml/½ pint milk
salt and freshly ground pepper
a pinch of grated nutmeg
2 eggs, beaten
3 × 15ml spoons/3 tablespoons kefalotiri or Parmesan cheese, grated

Put the sliced aubergine into a colander and sprinkle with salt. Leave to drain for about 30 minutes. Rinse them in water, drain thoroughly and dry on kitchen paper.

Put the flour in a bag, add the aubergine slices a few at a time and shake to coat them.

Heat 5 × 15ml spoons/5 tablespoons of oil in a heavy based pan and, when almost smoking hot, fry the aubergine slices over moderate heat a few at a time, in a single layer, turning them to brown them evenly on both sides. Add more oil for successive batches.

Add more oil and fry the onions, stirring frequently, until they turn light brown. Add the lamb and stir it for several minutes until it browns evenly. Stir in the tomatoes, tomato purée, garlic and herb, season with the cinnamon, salt and pepper and bring to the boil. Simmer the meat sauce for 20–25 minutes until most of the liquid has evaporated or been absorbed.

To make the egg sauce, melt the butter, stir in the flour and when it forms a smooth paste gradually pour on the milk, stirring constantly. Season with salt, pepper and nutmeg. Bring to the boil and simmer for 2 minutes, then allow to cool slightly and beat in the eggs.

To assemble the dish, cover the base of a shallow baking dish with one-third of the aubergine slices. Cover with half the meat mixture. Make another layer of aubergine, then one of all the remaining meat, then the rest of the aubergines. Pour the sauce on top and sprinkle with the cheese.

Stand the dish on a baking tray and cook in the oven at 190°C/375°F/Gas 5 for 35–40 minutes, until the top is well browned.

Hirino me Selino
Pork and Celery Casserole

Serves 4–6

---

2 heads celery
salt and freshly ground pepper
1kg/2¼ lb lean boneless pork, such as
  shoulder
4 × 15ml spoons/4 tablespoons lemon juice
5 × 15ml spoons/5 tablespoons olive oil

1 large onion, peeled and chopped
600ml/1 pint water
2 eggs
2 × 15ml spoons/2 tablespoons chopped
  coriander or parsley to garnish

Trim the celery, discarding any discoloured or stringy outer leaves, and wash it well. Cut each head through into 4cm/1½ in slices. Cook the celery in boiling, salted water for 10–15 minutes, until it is just tender. Drain and set aside.

Sprinkle the pork with 1 × 15ml spoon/1 tablespoon of the lemon juice. Heat 2 × 15ml spoons/2 tablespoons of the oil in a flameproof casserole and fry the meat, a few pieces at a time, over moderate heat. Turn the meat frequently to brown it evenly on all sides. Lift out the meat with a draining spoon, and add more oil for successive batches. When it is all cooked lift it out and set it aside.

Add the onions to the dish and fry them for 3–4 minutes, stirring once or twice. Pour on the water, stir well and bring to the boil.

Return the meat to the dish, bring the liquid to the boil again, cover and simmer for 1 hour. Add the celery, season with salt and pepper, return to the boil, cover and simmer for 20 minutes, or until the meat is tender.

Beat the egg with the remaining lemon juice. Add about 5 × 15ml spoons/5 tablespoons of the hot, but not boiling, stock and stir well. Tip the lemon mixture into the dish, stir well and heat gently. Taste and adjust seasoning if necessary.

Sprinkle with the chopped herb to garnish.

Mossharaki me Kremithia Stifado
Braised Beef

Serves 4–6

The Greek version of braised beef – the addition of cinnamon stick is what makes it special.

4 × 15ml spoons/4 tablespoons olive oil
1kg/2¼ lb lean stewing beef, cut into 5cm/2 in cubes
2 large tomatoes, skinned and sliced
5 × 15ml spoons/5 tablespoons tomato purée
450ml/¾ pint water

2 × 15ml spoons/2 tablespoons red wine vinegar
salt and freshly ground pepper
5cm/2 in piece of cinnamon stick
675g/1½ lb button onions, peeled and whole

Heat half the oil in a large flameproof casserole and fry the meat, a few pieces at a time, over moderate heat, turning it frequently until it browns evenly on all sides. Lift out the meat with a draining spoon and fry the remaining meat in more oil. Set the meat aside.

Add the tomatoes, tomato purée, water and vinegar to the casserole, season with salt and pepper, add the cinnamon and stir well. Bring to the boil. Return the meat to the casserole, cover the dish and simmer over low heat for 1¼ hours.

Blanch the onions in boiling water for 1 minute to 'mellow' them. Drain and add them to the casserole. Continue cooking for 30 minutes, or until the beef is tender. Taste and adjust seasoning if necessary. Discard the cinnamon.

Sofrito
Stewed Steak

A simple but aromatic way to cook lean beef, a speciality of the island of Corfu.

1kg/2¼ lb stewing steak, cut into 1cm/½ in thick 'finger' slices
4 × 15ml spoons/4 tablespoons flour
salt and freshly ground pepper
1 × 5ml spoon/1 teaspoon dried thyme flowers or leaves
6 × 15ml spoons/6 tablespoons red wine vinegar

6 × 15ml spoons/6 tablespoons water
2 garlic cloves, peeled and crushed
1 × 15ml spoon/1 tablespoon tomato purée
1 × 15ml spoon/1 tablespoon chopped parsley to garnish

Toss the meat in the flour seasoned with salt, pepper and the thyme.
Heat half of the oil and fry half the meat over moderate heat, turning it to brown it evenly. Lift out the meat, heat the remaining oil and fry the rest of the meat in the same way. Return the first batch of meat to the pan.
Pour on the vinegar and water, add the garlic cloves and stir in the tomato purée. Bring to the boil, cover the pan and simmer very gently for 1¼ hours, or until the meat is tender, adding a little more water if necessary.
Taste, and adjust the seasoning if needed. Sprinkle with the parsley to garnish.
Serve with sauté potatoes or fried potatoes – sorry, but they do these days.

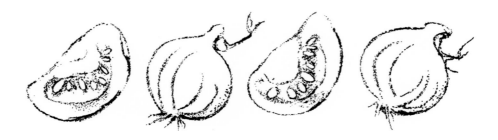

Soudzoukakia
Beef 'Sausages'

Serves 4

Not really a sausage – as they don't have skins – more of a rissole, spiced with cumin, flavoured with garlic, and simmered in tomato sauce.

75g/3 oz white bread, crumbled
450g/1 lb lean beef, minced
3 garlic cloves, peeled and crushed
1 small onion, peeled and grated
2 × 5ml spoons/2 teaspoons cumin seeds, crushed
salt and freshly ground pepper
1 egg, beaten

5 × 15ml spoons/5 tablespoons white wine
flour for coating
1 × 5ml spoon/1 teaspoon dried thyme
3 × 15ml spoons/3 tablespoons oil for shallow frying
300ml/½ pint Tomato sauce to serve (see page 29)

Soak the bread in water for about 15 minutes, then squeeze it dry.
Mash the minced meat with a wooden spoon (or work it in a food processor if you have one) until it forms a moist paste. If you don't do this the sausages will disintegrate.
Mix together the bread, meat, garlic, onion and cumin and season with salt and pepper. Beat in the egg and stir in the wine. Mix thoroughly and then knead with your hands until the mixture is smooth.
Shape into 'sausages' and coat them in flour seasoned with salt, pepper and thyme.
Heat the oil and fry the sausages over moderate heat for about 10 minutes, turning them to brown them evenly.
Pour on the tomato sauce, bring to the boil and simmer, uncovered, for 10 minutes.
Serve with rice or pasta.

Soudzoukakia, a kind of skinless beef
'sausage'

Kotopitta me Avga
Chicken and Egg Pie

Serves 6

In island houses where I have stayed the pie is prepared in the morning, soon after sunrise, the scent of the herbs mingling with the breakfast coffee. Then it is baked in the cool of the evening and served warm.

1.5kg/3¼ lb oven-ready chicken
3–4 stalks thyme
3–4 stalks parsley
2 bay leaves
1 small onion, peeled and sliced
1 stalk celery, sliced
salt and black peppercorns
SAUCE:
40g/1½ oz butter
40g/1½ oz flour

150ml/¼ pint milk
a pinch of ground coriander
2 × 15ml spoons/2 tablespoons chopped fresh
*   coriander or parsley*
3 eggs
40g/1½ oz walnuts, chopped
PASTRY:
40g/1½ oz butter, melted
225g/8 oz filo pastry

Put the chicken in a large pan, cover with water and add the herbs, onion, celery, salt and peppercorns. Bring to the boil and skim off any foam that rises to the surface. Cover and simmer for 1–1¼ hours, until the chicken is tender. Remove the chicken and strain the stock. Skin the chicken, cut the meat from the bones and cut it into cubes.

To make the sauce, melt the 40g/1½ oz butter in a small pan and stir in the flour. When it forms a smooth paste, gradually pour on 450ml/¾ pint of the reserved stock and the milk, stirring constantly. Bring to the boil and simmer for 3 minutes. Season the sauce with salt, pepper and ground coriander and stir in the chopped herb. Add the chicken, set aside to cool, then beat in the eggs and walnuts.

Brush a 33 × 23cm/13 × 9 in baking dish with melted butter. Spread half the pastry sheets to cover the base of the tin, brushing each one with butter. Spread the chicken mixture over the pastry. Cover with the remaining pastry, brushing each sheet and the top with butter. Just before baking sprinkle the top with water.

Bake the pie in the oven at 220°C/425°F/ Gas 7 for 10 minutes. Reduce the heat to 190°C/375°F/Gas 5 and continue baking for 25–30 minutes, until the top is well browned. Allow to cool slightly, then cut into squares to serve.

Serve with a mixed green salad or Spinach salad (see page 76).

Kota Kapama
Chicken in Cinnamon Sauce

Serves 4

The simple addition of a stick of cinnamon transforms the tomato sauce from ordinary to wonderful.

1–1.4kg/3 lb oven-ready chicken, quartered
½ lemon
salt and freshly ground pepper
3 × 15ml spoons/3 tablespoons olive oil
40g/1½ oz butter
2 medium onions, peeled and chopped

3 garlic cloves, peeled and chopped
2 stalks celery, chopped
2 × 15ml spoons/2 tablespoons tomato purée
1 × 400g/1 × 14 oz can tomatoes, chopped
4 × 15ml spoons/4 tablespoons red wine
12.5cm/5 in piece cinnamon stick

Rub the chicken all over with lemon and season it with salt and pepper. Heat the oil and butter in a large frying pan. Fry the chicken pieces over moderate heat for about 10 minutes to brown them evenly on all sides. Remove the chicken and set aside.
Add the onions, garlic and celery to the pan and fry for 5 minutes, stirring occasionally, until the vegetables begin to turn light brown. Stir in the tomato purée, tomatoes and wine, season with salt and pepper and add the cinnamon. Return the chicken to the pan, bring the sauce to the boil and cover the pan. Simmer for 45 minutes, or until the chicken is tender. Discard the cinnamon, taste the sauce and adjust the seasoning.
Lift out the chicken on to a heated serving dish and boil the sauce to reduce it slightly.
Serve with rice or pasta.

Lagos me Saltsa Karithia
Braised Hare in Walnut Sauce

Serves 4

Autumn in the Greek islands means two things to me – the piff-puff of the sporting guns and the tap-tap of people cracking walnut shells, straight from the trees. Here game and nuts come together in a dish that truly epitomizes 'the fat of the land'.

1 medium hare, cut into serving pieces
1 onion, peeled and sliced
3 × 15ml spoons/3 tablespoons vinegar
6 × 15ml spoons/6 tablespoons olive oil
70g/3½ oz butter
300ml/½ pint water
150ml/¼ pint red wine
4 × 15ml spoons/4 tablespoons lemon juice
salt and freshly ground pepper

½ × 5ml spoon/½ teaspoon ground
    cinnamon
3 bay leaves
150g/5 oz walnuts, shelled and crushed
1 × 15ml spoon/1 tablespoon flour
3 × 15ml spoons/3 tablespoons brandy
    (optional)
6 medium slices bread, crusts removed
coriander or parsley sprigs to garnish

Soak the hare overnight in a bowl of water with the onion and vinegar. Drain and dry the hare.

Heat the oil and 40g/1½ oz of the butter in a flameproof casserole and fry the hare over moderate heat for about 15 minutes, until it is evenly brown on all sides. Pour on the water, wine and lemon juice, season with salt, pepper and cinnamon and add the bay leaves.

Cover the casserole and simmer for 2 hours, or until the hare is tender. Stir together the walnuts and flour and stir the mixture into the stock. Stir in the brandy if using. Simmer for 5 minutes. Taste the sauce and adjust the seasoning if needed.

Melt the remaining butter and fry the bread on both sides until it is well browned and dry. Cut it into triangles and arrange them on a serving dish. Place the hare on the bread and pour the sauce over. Garnish with the coriander or parsley.

Perdikes Yiouvetsi
Partridge with Pasta

Serves 4

We once went into a taverna on the island of Nissiros, in the Dodecanese, and asked if – as it was rather late – it would be possible to have lunch. 'Yes,' said the proprietor, 'as long as you don't mind only spaghetti.' The 'only spaghetti' came in a huge mound, and well hidden underneath it (as it was out of the shooting season) was a whole partridge.

2 dressed partridges
50g/2 oz butter
1 head celery, trimmed and sliced
1 large onion, peeled and sliced
450g/1 lb tomatoes, skinned and sliced
1 × 15ml spoon/1 tablespoon red wine
  vinegar
150ml/¼ pint water

2 bay leaves
2 × 15ml spoons/2 tablespoons chopped
  marjoram or 2 × 5ml spoons/2 teaspoons
  dried oregano
salt and freshly ground pepper
350g/12 oz spaghetti
4 × 15ml spoons/4 tablespoons double cream

Melt the butter in a flameproof casserole and fry the partridges over moderate heat for 10–15 minutes, turning frequently to brown them evenly. Lift out the birds.

Add the celery and onion and fry for 2–3 minutes, stirring. Add the tomatoes, vinegar, water and herbs and season with salt and pepper. Bring to the boil, return the partridges to the dish, cover and simmer slowly for 45 minutes, turning the birds at least once.

Cook the spaghetti in boiling, salted water for 10–12 minutes, or according to the directions on the packet, until it is just tender. Drain it into a colander, run hot water through it and drain again.

Transfer the birds to a heated serving dish. Taste the sauce and adjust the seasoning if necessary. If it is too liquid fast-boil it to reduce it slightly, then stir in the cream.

Spoon the spaghetti around the partridges and spoon the sauce over it.

DAIRY PRODUCE

I never think of Greek dairies as acres of highly-scrubbed, highly automated processing plant, though doubtless there must be some of these, where they produce all that delicious yoghurt.

To my mind the Greek 'dairy' is right out there on the hillside. It's a friendly old lady sitting under the shade of an olive tree and looking up occasionally when her goats or a visitor amble past. It's a farmer jogging his way home on a donkey, while the goats trot skittishly along behind. It's a flock of sheep grazing hopefully beside a dried-up river bed. And countless homely kitchens with pans of yoghurt, nets of draining curds and blocks of maturing cheese.

If you have designs on creating at least part of this atmosphere, it's the easiest thing in the world to make your own yoghurt, and to make a quite acceptable curd cheese by straining it. If you can't go to the lengths of keeping your own goat, at least there are more and more people who do, and thus far more chances to buy goat's milk.

One word of caution: don't buy frozen goat's milk (the form in which it is most widely available) and expect fabulous yoghurt. Mine has never set properly, and always separated, so it's important – and well worthwhile – to search out a source of supply for fresh milk.

Yaourti
Yoghurt

Makes 1 litre/1¾ pints

Chatting to a goatherd on Samos once, I mentioned how much I wished we could make real Greek yoghurt at home. 'Well,' he said. 'It's easy. All you have to do is buy some goats. Let them eat all the flowers and vegetables in your garden. And of course get up at four in the morning to milk them. No problem!' Point taken!

1 litre/1¾ pints goat's milk

2 × 15ml spoons/2 tablespoons plain, live yoghurt

Heat the milk to just below boiling point, then take it off the heat and leave it to cool to blood heat (when it feels only slightly warm when you dip a finger in).

Gradually pour the milk over the yoghurt, stirring all the time. Either pour it into a wide-necked vacuum flask and close the lid or pour it into a bowl or a number of small pots, cover and leave in a warm place (such as the top of the cooker or on the boiler) for 5–6 hours, until it is set.

Store the yoghurt in the refrigerator for up to 6 days.

As time goes on, the yoghurt will begin to taste slightly bitter, but there is no need to leave it so long. It's delicious for breakfast, sprinkled with sugar or stirred with honey; it can be used as a sauce or marinade with meat, fish and vegetables; it has just the right acid content for bread and scones; stirred with cucumber or mint it makes a cooling salad; it combines perfectly with cheese and other savoury ingredients in dips; it can replace cream in puddings, and can even be strained to make a type of curd cheese.

Kolokythaki Soufflé
Courgette Soufflé

Serves 4

Courgettes and marrows are prolific in Greece and are served every which-way. This is a popular, though of course not exactly local dish, which I was first offered sitting beside a donkey and a waterfall on a by-road on Andros.

350g/12 oz courgettes or marrow, trimmed and sliced
75g/3 oz butter
50g/2 oz flour
300ml/½ pint milk
75g/3 oz kefalotiri or Parmesan cheese, grated

4 × 15ml spoons/4 tablespoons chopped fresh coriander or parsley
4 eggs, separated
salt and freshly ground pepper

Peel marrow, but not young courgettes. Steam the vegetable over boiling water until tender, then chop it finely.

Melt the butter, stir in the flour and gradually pour on the milk, stirring constantly. Bring to the boil and simmer for 3 minutes. Remove the pan from the heat. Stir in the chopped vegetable, cheese and herb.

Beat in the egg yolks, and season the mixture with salt and pepper. Whisk the whites until they stand in stiff peaks, and fold them in.

Pre-heat the oven to 200°C/400°F/Gas 6. Pour the mixture into a greased 1 litre/2 pint soufflé dish and bake for 40 minutes, until the soufflé is well risen.

Serve at once with a mixed salad.

Courgette Soufflé and Country Salad
(page 73)

Omeleta me Patates
Potato Omelette

Serves 4

Another speciality from my friend Adonis, on Andros. You can't imagine his simple pride as he puts the massive black frying pan on to the centre of the table and lovingly sprinkles olive oil and herbs on top.

225g/8 oz young green beans, topped and
tailed
175g/6 oz butter
450g/1 lb potatoes, peeled and thinly sliced
salt and freshly ground pepper
10 eggs, beaten

2 × 15ml spoons/2 tablespoons chopped mint
4 × 15ml spoons/4 tablespoons double cream
2 × 15ml spoons/2 tablespoons olive oil
2 × 15ml spoons/2 tablespoons chopped
marjoram or parsley

Blanch the beans in boiling water for 3 minutes. Drain them and toss them on kitchen paper to dry.

Melt half the butter in a large frying-pan, add the potatoes and beans, season with salt and pepper, cover and cook over low heat for 15–20 minutes until the vegetables are tender and have absorbed the butter.

Beat the mint and cream into the eggs, season with salt and pepper and pour over the vegetables. Increase the heat to moderate and cook for 3–4 minutes, until the omelette is set. Slide it on to a heated plate, invert it and return the omelette to the pan, the other way up. Cook it to brown the second side.

Sprinkle oil and the herb over the omelette and cut into wedges to serve. Serve with a mixed salad.

Psiti Crema
Baked Custard

Serves 4

It's the cinnamon that makes these custards so distinctively and deliciously Greek.

6 egg yolks
75g/3 oz sugar

450ml/¾ pint plain yoghurt
ground cinnamon

Beat together the egg yolks and sugar until pale and creamy. Gradually beat in the yoghurt and continue beating until the mixture is smooth.
Pour the mixture into 4 individual soufflé dishes and sprinkle each one generously with cinnamon. Stand the dishes in a roasting pan with water to come half-way up the sides. Bake in the oven at 180°C/350°F/Gas 4 for 30 minutes, until the custards are set. Remove from the oven and stand on a wire rack to cool.
Serve chilled, with fresh fruit.

Yaourtopitta me Lemono
Lemon and Yoghurt Cake

Serves 8

100g/4 oz butter
175g/6 oz sugar
2 × 15ml spoons/2 tablespoons grated lemon
  rind
3 eggs, separated
175g/6 oz plain white flour

175ml/6 fl oz plain yoghurt
75g/3 oz candied lemon peel, chopped
ICING:
about 100g/4 oz icing sugar, sifted
1 × 15ml spoon/1 tablespoon lemon juice

Cream the butter and sugar until light and fluffy, then beat in the lemon rind. Beat in the egg yolks one at a time and add the sifted flour alternately with the yoghurt. Stir in the chopped peel.
Whisk the egg whites until they are stiff and fold them into the mixture. Pre-heat the oven to 180°C/350°F/Gas 4. Turn the mixture into a greased loaf tin and bake for 1 hour, until well risen and golden brown. Cool the cake slightly in the tin, then turn it out on to a wire rack to become cold.
To make the frosting, stir the lemon juice into the icing sugar and spread it over the cake.

Yaourtopitta me Meli
Yoghurt and Honey Cake

Serves 8–10

The Greeks have an almost unique reputation for liking extra-sweet things. Serving this cake with plain yoghurt, though not typical, makes it seem less rich.

3 eggs
200g/7 oz sugar
250ml/8 fl oz plain yoghurt plus extra to serve
225g/8 oz plain white flour
1 × 5ml spoon/1 teaspoon ground cinnamon

1 × 5ml spoon/1 teaspoon bicarbonate of soda
1 × 15ml spoon/1 tablespoon lemon juice
SYRUP:
225g/8 oz honey
150ml/¼ pint water

Beat the eggs and sugar until the mixture is pale and creamy, then stir in the yoghurt. Sift together the flour and cinnamon and fold into the mixture. Stir the bicarbonate of soda into the lemon juice and quickly stir it into the cake mixture, which will froth for a few moments.

Pre-heat the oven to 180°C/350°F/Gas 4. Turn the mixture into a greased rectangular cake tin and bake for 45–50 minutes, until the cake is well risen.

Meanwhile, melt the honey and water, bring to the boil and simmer for 5 minutes. Set aside to cool.

Stand the cake tin on a wire rack and, while it is still hot, pour on the syrup. Don't worry that the cake will sink a little.

Allow the cake to cool, then serve it, cut into squares, with the yoghurt. And forks, as it's very sticky.

Potato Omelette (page 64)

Crema
Cornflour and Nut Pudding

Serves 6

1 litre/1¾ pints creamy milk
50g/2 oz cornflour
75g/3 oz sugar
3 egg yolks

2 × 5ml spoons/2 teaspoons grated orange rind
2 × 5ml spoons/2 teaspoons vanilla essence
4 × 15ml spoons/4 tablespoons pistachio nuts, chopped

Heat the milk until it is almost boiling. Mix together the cornflour, sugar, egg yolks, orange rind and vanilla. Pour on a little of the hot milk, stir well and pour the egg mixture into the pan, or into the top of a double boiler over a pan of simmering water.
Cook the custard over very low heat, stirring all the time, until it thickens – about 20 minutes.
Pour the pudding into a serving dish, or into individual dishes, and leave to cool. Sprinkle with the nuts just before serving.

Rizogalo
Cinnamon Rice Pudding

Serves 6

1 litre/1¾ pints creamy milk
5 × 15ml spoons/5 tablespoons sugar
4 × 15ml spoons/4 tablespoons short-grain rice

a strip of thinly pared lemon rind
3 egg yolks, beaten
4 × 15ml spoons/4 tablespoons double cream
1 × 5ml spoon/1 teaspoon ground cinnamon

Put the milk, sugar, rice and lemon rind into a pan and stir over low heat to dissolve the sugar. Bring slowly to the boil and simmer for about 45 minutes, or until the rice is tender and has absorbed all the milk. Discard the lemon peel. Cool slightly.
Beat in the egg yolks and cream and stir over very low heat for 2–3 minutes. Do not allow the mixture to boil or the eggs will curdle.
Pour into a serving dish, leave to cool and then sprinkle with the cinnamon. Serve cold.

Galatoboureko
Cream Pie

Serves 10–12

There are specialist pastry shops in every Greek town, and there's no better way to judge them than by the quality of their creamy custard pies. Some recipes use only lemon for flavouring, but my vote goes to the spiced version.

1 litre/1¾ pints milk
1 stick cinnamon
3 eggs
225g/8 oz sugar
75g/3 oz semolina
½ × 5ml spoon/½ teaspoon ground cinnamon

PASTRY:
225g/8 oz filo pastry
100g/4 oz butter, melted
SYRUP:
225g/8 oz sugar
600ml/1 pint water
1 stick cinnamon

Heat the milk with the cinnamon stick until just below boiling point. Beat the eggs and sugar until light and creamy. Stir in the semolina and ground cinnamon and gradually pour on the milk. Pour the mixture into the pan and simmer over very low heat, stirring constantly, until it thickens. On no account allow it to boil, or the eggs will scramble. Remove the custard from the heat, discard the cinnamon and stir the custard until it cools – otherwise it is quite likely to set in unattractive lumps.

Brush a 23 × 19cm/9 × 7 in baking tray with melted butter and cover it with a sheet of pastry large enough to slightly overhang the tin on all sides. Brush the pastry with butter and continue adding more sheets, until you have used half.

Pour in the custard mixture and level the top. Fold over the sides of the pastry and cover the pie with the remaining sheets, brushing each one with melted butter. Brush the top thoroughly with butter and mark into squares, cutting almost through to the filling.

Set the oven at 190°C/375°F/Gas 5 and bake the pie for 1 hour, or until the top is well browned.

To make the syrup, put the sugar, water and cinnamon into a pan and stir over low heat until the sugar has dissolved. Bring to the boil and boil for 20 minutes, until the syrup thickens. Remove the cinnamon.

Stand the pie on a wire rack and, while it is still hot, pour the hot syrup over. Leave to cool.

SALADS & VEGETABLES

Visitors to Greece, offered time and again the ubiquitous 'horiatikisalata' of peppers, cucumber and tomatoes, could be forgiven for failing to realize that in fact vegetables, in a wide variety, represent a major and important part of the nation's diet. This is partly because of habit formed by centuries of strict religious fasting, and partly for economic reasons. Unfortunately, the taverna owners on the tourist run don't seem to have 'got the message', and seldom serve the more interesting vegetable dishes.

I especially enjoy the pilaffs made with vegetables such as tomatoes, courgettes or spinach stirred into the rice – so much more interesting than rice alone. Stuffed vegetables are a special delight – and these you do find in restaurants. Purplish-black aubergine shells (they call them 'little shoes') filled with lentils, glowing red tomatoes brimming over with herby rice, marrow packed with rice and cheese – all are worthy of a course to themselves.

In the country districts gathering wild greens isn't a pastime to give the rabbits a treat – it's for supper. The Greek way with greens is to simmer them in water and toss them in an oil dressing or to cook them – very, very lightly – in a mixture of oil and water. Either way, the leaves emerge glistening, shiny-bright and irresistible. And well worth copying. Taverna owners, please note!

Rizi Pilafi me Spanaki
Spinach Pilaff

Serves 4

This 'green rice' makes an attractive accompaniment to tomato-based casseroles and to roast and grilled meats.

675g/1½ lb spinach
150ml/¼ pint olive oil
2 medium onions, peeled and chopped
175g/6 oz short-grain rice, washed and
drained
450ml/¾ pint chicken stock

1 × 15ml spoon/1 tablespoon lemon juice
salt and freshly ground pepper
25g/1 oz butter
2 × 15ml spoons/2 tablespoons kefalotiri or
Parmesan cheese, grated

Tear off the tough stalks from the spinach, tear the leaves into pieces and wash and drain them well.

Heat the oil in a large pan and fry the onions over moderate heat for 3–4 minutes, stirring once or twice. Add the rice and stir-fry it for 1 minute. Pour on the stock and lemon juice, season with salt and pepper, stir well and bring to the boil. Cover the pan and simmer over low heat for 10 minutes.

Stir in the spinach, cover and continue cooking for 10 minutes, until the rice is tender and has absorbed the liquid, and the spinach has collapsed.

Stir in the butter, cover and set aside for 5 minutes before serving. Sprinkle with the cheese.

Papoutsakia
Baked Stuffed Aubergines

Serves 4

'Little Shoes', as they are called, can have a variety of fillings with or without meat. This meatless version draws attention to the perfect partnership of the aubergines and the other vegetables.

100g/4 oz brown continental lentils, soaked for about 2 hours and drained
2 medium aubergines, about 400g/14 oz each
salt and freshly ground pepper
6 × 15ml spoons/6 tablespoons olive oil
1 medium onion, peeled and finely chopped
1 garlic clove, peeled and finely chopped
2 stalks tender celery, finely chopped
2 medium carrots, finely chopped
2 large tomatoes, skinned and chopped

2 × 15ml spoons/2 tablespoons tomato purée
2 × 15ml spoons/2 tablespoons chopped parsley
300ml/½ pint chicken stock
TOPPING:
150ml/¼ pint plain yoghurt
2 eggs, beaten
50g/2 oz kefalotiri or Parmesan cheese, grated

Trim the stalk ends from the aubergines and halve them lengthways. Using a spoon or a vegetable baller, scoop out the flesh, leaving firm 'walls'. Chop the flesh and place it in a colander. Sprinkle both the aubergines shells and the chopped flesh with salt and set aside to drain for about 45 minutes. Rinse and dry thoroughly.

Heat half the oil in a pan and fry the aubergine shells over moderate heat for about 5 minutes on each side. Remove them from the pan and set them aside. Heat the remaining oil and fry the onion, garlic, celery and carrot over moderate heat for 4–5 minutes, stirring once or twice. Stir in the lentils, chopped aubergines, tomatoes, tomato purée and parsley, pour on the stock and bring to the boil. Cover and simmer for 45 minutes, until the lentils are tender and have absorbed the stock. If there is any excess liquid, increase the heat and fast-boil the mixture to evaporate it. Taste the filling and adjust the seasoning if necessary.

Place the aubergines in a greased baking dish that just fits them. Spoon in the filling, packing it in tightly.

Beat together the yoghurt and eggs, stir in the cheese and season with salt and pepper. Pour the topping over the aubergines.

Bake, uncovered, in the oven at 190°C/375°F/Gas 5 for 40–45 minutes, until the topping is well risen and deep brown.

Serve hot, warm or cold.

Domatasalata
Tomato Salad

Serves 4

The traditional way to serve tomato salad is simply with an oil dressing, like this.

450g/1 lb tomatoes, sliced
1 large onion, peeled and thinly sliced into rings
150ml/¼ pint olive oil

salt and freshly ground pepper
2 × 15ml spoons/2 tablespoons chopped fresh coriander or mint

Arrange the tomatoes and onions on a dish. Season the oil with salt and pepper and pour over the salad. Scatter with the chopped herb. To decorate the salad, add a few sprigs of fresh herb.

Horiatikisalata
Greek Country Salad

Serves 4

This must be the best-known Greek dish of all – thanks to taverna owners the length and breadth of the land. Even so, it's actually very nice, served as part of the mezethes, with any main dish, or as a course in its own right.

1 green pepper, trimmed, cored and seeded and sliced into rings
1 medium onion, peeled and thinly sliced
350g/12 oz tomatoes, thinly sliced into wedges
1 medium cucumber, thickly sliced, then quartered

100g/4 oz feta cheese, very thinly sliced
75g/3 oz black olives
DRESSING:
6 × 15ml spoons/6 tablespoons olive oil
salt and freshly ground pepper
1 × 5ml spoon/1 teaspoon dried oregano

Put the pepper, onion, tomatoes and cucumber into a dish. Some people serve the salad in layers, others toss it – it's up to you. Arrange the cheese slices and olives on top.
Season the oil with salt, pepper and the dried oregano and drizzle the dressing over the salad.

Domates Yemistes Nistisimes
Baked Stuffed Tomatoes

Serves 4

Whenever you are invited into the kitchen of a taverna to select your meal, there is invariably a round metal dish of toasty-brown-topped tomatoes. Serve them, cold or warm, as a light meal with salad, or to accompany meat or fish.

8 large tomatoes
salt and freshly ground pepper
6 × 15ml spoons/6 tablespoons olive oil
1 large onion, peeled and finely chopped
2 garlic cloves, peeled and finely chopped
150g/6 oz cooked long-grain rice

6 × 15ml spoons/6 tablespoons chopped mint
6 × 15ml spoons/6 tablespoons tomato purée
50g/2 oz feta cheese, finely crumbled (or use ricotta)
6 × 15ml spoons/6 tablespoons water
1 × 15ml spoon/1 tablespoon dried oregano

Cut a slice from the top of each tomato and, using a teaspoon or vegetable baller, scoop out the flesh and seeds, taking care not to pierce the walls. Sprinkle the insides of the tomatoes with salt and turn them upside down on a plate to drain for about 30 minutes. Chop the tomato flesh.

Heat the oil and fry the onion and garlic over moderate heat for 3–4 minutes, stirring once or twice. Stir in the chopped tomato, rice, mint and half of the tomato purée and season with salt and pepper. Bring the mixture to the boil and cook for 4–5 minutes, stirring. Taste the mixture and season with a little more pepper if needed (do not add more salt as the cheese is often quite salty). Stir in the cheese and remove from the heat.

Rinse the tomatoes under cold, running water, drain and dry them. Place them in a greased baking dish which just fits them. Spoon in the filling, piling it up to a mound.

Mix the remaining tomato purée with the water, season with salt and pepper and stir in the oregano. Pour the sauce around the tomatoes.

Bake in the oven at 190°C/375°F/Gas 5 for 20–25 minutes until the tops are well browned.

Serve warm or cold.

Baked Stuffed Tomatoes and Bean Salad
(page 77)

Spanaki-salata
Spinach Salad

Serves 4

Lightly cooked spinach, prepared in just the way it is to serve as a vegetable, is cooled to make a glistening and tasty salad.

1kg/2¼ lb spinach
5 × 15ml spoons/5 tablespoons olive oil
1 medium onion, peeled and sliced

salt and freshly ground pepper
2 × 15ml spoons/2 tablespoons lemon juice
1 lemon, quartered, to serve

Tear the tough stalks from the spinach and tear large leaves into 2 or 3 pieces. Wash the spinach thoroughly and drain it.
Heat the oil and fry the onion for 10 minutes over low heat, stirring frequently. Add the spinach and season with salt and pepper. Stir well with a wooden spoon to coat the leaves with oil. Cover the pan and cook over moderately low heat for about 7 minutes, until the spinach is tender but has not collapsed. Sprinkle with the lemon juice and grind on more pepper.
Serve warm, or cold as a salad, with lemon wedges.

Revythia-salata
Chick Pea Salad

Serves 4

225g/8 oz dried chick peas, soaked overnight
  and drained
salt
1 medium onion, peeled and finely chopped
3 stalks tender celery, thinly sliced
2 × 15ml spoons/2 tablespoons chopped
  parsley

sprigs of coriander or parsley to garnish
DRESSING:
6–7 × 15ml spoons/6–7 tablespoons olive oil
2 × 15ml spoons/2 tablespoons red wine
  vinegar
freshly ground pepper
1 garlic clove, peeled and finely chopped

Cook the chick peas in a pan of boiling, unsalted water for 1½ hours, then add salt and cook for a further 30 minutes, or until tender. Drain the peas.
Mix together the dressing ingredients and pour them over the peas while they are still warm. Toss well, then set aside to cool.
Stir in the onion, celery and parsley. Garnish with the herb sprigs.

Fassolia-salata
Bean Salad

Serves 4

450g/1 lb young green beans, topped and
    tailed
salt
1 small onion, peeled and thinly sliced into
    rings
1 lemon, quartered, to serve

DRESSING:
5 × 15ml spoons/5 tablespoons olive oil
2 × 15ml spoons/2 tablespoons lemon juice
1 garlic clove, peeled and crushed
freshly ground pepper

Cook the beans in boiling, salted water for 5 minutes, or until almost tender,
then drain them.
Pour the oil over the beans while they are still warm, and toss well. Set aside
to cool. Stir in the lemon juice and garlic and season with salt and pepper.
Turn out the beans on to a dish and scatter with the onion rings. Serve with
the lemon wedges.

Radikya-salata
Dandelion Salad

Serves 4

Wild vegetable salads, the food for free from the countryside, are an almost everyday
accompaniment to meat and fish dishes. If you have young dandelion leaves in the
garden, gather them for this tasty example.

450g/1 lb young dandelion leaves, washed
    and drained
salt
1 lemon, quartered, to serve

DRESSING:
6 × 15ml spoons/6 tablespoons olive oil
2 × 15ml spoons/2 tablespoons lemon juice
freshly ground pepper

Cook the leaves in boiling, salted water for 5 minutes, or until just tender.
Drain them into a colander and refresh them in ice-cold water. This prevents
further cooking and preserves their colour. Set them aside to cool, then toss
them on kitchen paper to dry.
Mix the dressing ingredients. Turn the leaves into a serving dish, pour on the
dressing and toss well. Serve with the lemon wedges.

Kolokithi tis Androu
Andros Marrow

Serves 4–6

I first tasted this country vegetable dish at a nunnery – a welcome reward for a long, hard climb. Next, with some revisions, I cooked it with my hostess, Maria, in her kitchen behind the wine shop on the harbour front.

1 medium marrow
2 × 15ml spoons/2 tablespoons olive oil
1 large onion, peeled and grated
1 litre/1¾ pints boiling water
175g/6 oz long-grain rice, washed and
  drained

salt and freshly ground pepper
6 × 15ml spoons/6 tablespoons chopped mint
75g/3 oz feta cheese, crumbled (or use ricotta)
12 canned or bottled vine leaves

Cut a slice from each end of the marrow. Using a spoon or vegetable baller, scoop out the seeds and stringy fibres. Trim the end slices to make 'plugs' to push into each end.

Put the oil, onion and 450ml/¾ pint of the water into a flameproof dish, bring to the boil and simmer for 10 minutes. Add the rice, salt, pepper and mint. Cover and simmer gently for 25 minutes, or until the rice has absorbed all the water. Stir in the cheese, then remove from the dish and set aside to cool.

Plug one end of the marrow with one of the trimmed slices and pack in the filling. Plug the other end of the marrow.

Pre-heat the oven to 180°C/350°F/Gas 4. Spread 6 vine leaves over the base of the dish, place the marrow on them and cover with the remaining leaves. Pour on the remaining 600ml/1 pint water and bake for 35–40 minutes, until the marrow is tender.

Serve with Tomato sauce (see page 29)

Note You can cook peeled and thinly sliced potatoes with this, placed around the marrow.

Andros Marrow served with Tomato Sauce
(page 29)

FESTIVAL FARE

Greece is a country of many traditions, festivals and thanksgivings, each one an occasion for the whole family to get together. Those who have left the islands or the countryside to work in the cities flock home, laden with plastic carrier bags and cardboard boxes, sure of a tearful reunion on the quayside or doorstep.

There is enough joy and pleasure to spare to embrace tourists, too, who are welcomed as honorary members of the community. In a village when there's a wedding you may be invited to sit down with the family to a meal of roast lamb in the taverna, drink to the happy couple from your neighbour's glass and bless the bride with a slice of pink meringue cake. When there's a christening every passer-by is offered a gift of sugared almonds in a twist of net, and when someone is celebrating his name-day, the day of his patron saint, everyone is invited to call in for a drink and a cake.

Easter is the highlight of the year, and even today the Lenten fast is strictly observed in many households, with meat, eggs and dairy products prohibited on certain days each week and, together with olive oil, for the whole of the week before Easter. That fast is traditionally broken after the church service, with lamb soup to be followed, later on Easter Sunday, by spit-roast Pascal lamb cooked and eaten out of doors – one of the many joys of the Greek way of life.

Galopoulo Yemisto me Kima
Turkey with Minced Meat Stuffing
Serves 12–16

In years gone by the Greeks ate roast pork for Christmas dinner, but now – reluctantly in many cases – they have adopted the general Western tradition, and it's turkey that takes pride of place.

1 oven-ready turkey, about 5kg/11–12 lb
salt and freshly ground pepper
1 lemon, halved
75g/3 oz butter, melted
STUFFING:
75g/3 oz butter
2 large onions, peeled and finely chopped
2 stalks tender celery, finely chopped
225g/8 oz minced veal

1 turkey liver and heart, minced
350g/12 oz chestnuts, boiled, shelled, peeled
  and chopped
100g/4 oz walnuts, chopped
75g/3 oz long-grain rice, washed and drained
300ml/½ pint turkey or chicken stock
50g/2 oz seedless raisins
1 cooking apple, peeled, cored and chopped

To make the stuffing, melt the butter in a large frying-pan and fry the onions and celery over moderate heat for 3–4 minutes, stirring once or twice. Stir in the minced veal and fry until lightly coloured. Stir in the minced liver and heart, the nuts and rice and pour on the stock. Bring to the boil, cover the pan and simmer for 10 minutes. Stir in the raisins and apple, season with salt and pepper and simmer for 5 minutes, or until there is no excess liquid. Set aside to cool.

Stuff the turkey with the meat mixture and sew up the cavities or close them with skewers. Tie the legs and wings, or secure them with skewers.

Season the turkey all over with salt and pepper, rub it with the lemon, then brush it with the melted butter.

Place the turkey in a roasting pan and cook it in the oven at 200°C/400°F/Gas 6 for 20 minutes, then reduce the temperature to 180°C/350°F/Gas 4 and cook for about 5 hours, basting frequently.

Test that it is cooked by piercing the thickest part of the thigh with a fine skewer. The juices should run clear.

Mayiritsa
Easter Soup
Serves 6–8

This is the first dish to break the Lenten fast, served when the churchgoers return from midnight mass on Holy Saturday. It is traditionally made from the entrails of the Pascal lamb; the following ingredients are a more practical alternative.

1kg/2¼ lb shoulder of lamb on the bone, trimmed of excess fat
1 large onion, peeled and sliced
a handful of fresh herbs
1kg/2¼ lb lamb's liver, heart and lights
50g/2 oz butter
12 spring onions, trimmed and sliced
2 cos lettuce hearts, shredded

12 × 15ml spoons/ 12 tablespoons chopped mixed herbs, such as fresh coriander, parsley and dill
salt and freshly ground pepper
75g/3 oz long-grain rice, washed and drained
SAUCE:
3 eggs
5 × 15ml spoons/5 tablespoons lemon juice

Chop the shoulder of lamb into 3 or 4 pieces and put it in a pan of water with the onion and bunch of herbs. Bring to the boil, skim off any foam that rises to the surface and cover the pan. Simmer for 1 hour. Lift out the lamb, cut the meat from the bones and cut it into bite-sized pieces. Discard the bones. Strain and reserve the stock.

Wash the offal and blanch it in boiling water for 1–2 minutes. Drain it and cut it into bite-sized pieces.

Melt the butter in a pan and fry the spring onions over moderate heat for 3–4 minutes, stirring once or twice. Add the sliced offal and stir-fry for 2–3 minutes. Stir in the lamb, lettuce and chopped herbs and pour on 1.5 litres/ 2½ pints of the reserved meat stock. Season with salt and pepper and bring to the boil. Again, skim off any foam that rises to the top. Cover the pan and simmer for 30 minutes.

Add the rice, return to the boil, cover and simmer for 10 minutes.

Beat the eggs, gradually beat in the lemon juice and a few spoons of the hot (but not boiling) stock. Pour the egg mixture into the pan and heat gently, without boiling. Taste the soup and adjust the seasoning if necessary.

Siko Gliko
Fig Sweetmeats

Serves 8–10

450g/1 lb dried figs (must be moist and juicy)
150g/6 oz walnut halves
3 × 15ml spoons/3 tablespoons clear honey

1 × 5ml spoon/1 teaspoon ground cinnamon
250ml/9 fl oz water

Split the figs almost in half and fill them with the walnuts. Arrange them in a single layer in a shallow baking dish which just fits them.
Dissolve the honey and cinnamon in the water and pour it over the figs.
Bake the dish, uncovered, in the oven at 180°C/350°F/Gas 4 for 20–25 minutes, until all the liquid has been absorbed.
The figs are delicious served hot, with plain yoghurt or single cream. Or leave them to cool and store them in an airtight container in the refrigerator.

Kourabiethes me Karithia
Walnut Shortbread

Makes about 20 biscuits

450g/1 lb plain white flour
1 × 5ml spoon/1 teaspoon baking powder
225g/8 oz unsalted butter, at room
    temperature
75g/3 oz caster sugar
1 × 5ml spoon/1 teaspoon vanilla essence

1 egg yolk
50g/2 oz chopped walnuts
about 75g/3 oz sifted icing sugar for dusting
about 1 × 15ml spoon/1 tablespoon rosewater
about 20 whole cloves

Sift the flour and baking powder. Cream the butter and sugar until light and creamy, then beat in the vanilla essence and egg yolk. Gradually beat in the flour, then stir in the walnuts. Shape the dough into a round and knead it lightly until free from cracks.
Break the dough into pieces slightly larger than a walnut and flatten them. Place them on a greased and floured baking sheet.
Bake the biscuits in the oven at 180°C/350°F/Gas 4 for 20 minutes, or until they are beginning to turn golden brown at the edges. Remove from the oven, and while still hot, dust them with icing sugar and sprinkle them with rosewater, then stick a clove in the centre of each. Transfer them to a wire rack to cool. Store in an airtight tin.

Vassilopitta
New Year Cake

Makes 1 large loaf

This light, sweet bread is traditionally served on New Year's Day. The cutting is all part of the ceremony. One slice is cut for Christ, then one for each member of the family. Excitement mounts, to see who is lucky enough to receive the hidden coin.

1kg/2¼ lb flour
1 × 5ml spoon/1 teaspoon salt
50g/2 oz fresh yeast
250ml/8 fl oz milk, lukewarm, plus extra for
  brushing

4 eggs
100g/4 oz sugar
225g/8 oz unsalted butter, softened
3 × 15ml spoons/3 tablespoons sesame seeds

Sift the flour and salt into a bowl. Crumble the yeast into the warm milk, stir in 4 × 15ml spoons/4 tablespoons of flour, cover the bowl and leave it in a warm place to become frothy.

Make a well in the centre of the flour and beat in the eggs one at a time. Beat in the sugar, melted butter and the yeast solution. Form the mixture into a dough and knead until smooth and elastic. Cover the dough with oiled polythene and leave it in a warm place for about 2 hours, or until it has doubled in bulk.

Knead the dough again on a lightly floured board for 5 minutes and press a coin into it. Shape the dough into a round and press it into an oiled 20cm/8 in cake tin. Cover and leave it in a warm place for a further 10 minutes.

Brush the top of the dough with milk and scatter on the sesame seeds. Preheat the oven to 190°C/375°F/Gas 5 and bake for 50 minutes, or until the bread sounds hollow when the base is tapped. Transfer it to a wire rack to cool.

PASTRIES & SWEETS

A small cup of thick, dark aromatic coffee, a sparkling glass of ice-cold water and a sticky pastry or 'spoon sweet' – what a perfect combination to while away a leisurely morning or afternoon, or to finish off a meal.

Visitors may glance around a restaurant or taverna in vain, looking to see if other guests are drinking coffee. Usually they are not. The trick is to go to a pastryshop, or kafenion, the commercial heart of this very pleasant ritual.

In Greek homes it is unthinkable to welcome a guest, on however short an acquaintance, without offering this simple but gracious form of hospitality.

A small diamond-shaped pastry oozing with nuts and honey and soaked in syrup; a few cubes of halva glinting with sugar and specked with colourful pistachios; a tiny glass or ceramic dish of fruit, any fruit, preserved in thick syrup; a pile of light-as-a-feather fritters sprinkled with nuts and cinnamon; fingers of creamy cake flavoured with the distinctive honey from Mount Hymettus – it's a question of 'when in Rome', or in this case Athens. And forget about the calories!

New Year Cake (page 85) and *Walnut Shortbread (page 84)*

Baklava
Nut Pastries

Makes about 24

These pastries, which you find in every pastryshop in Greece, look complicated, but once you get into the rhythm of brushing and layering the pastry it's surprising how simple they are.

450g/1lb filo pastry
150g/6 oz unsalted butter, melted
FILLING:
4 × 15ml spoons/4 tablespoons honey
2 × 15ml spoons/2 tablespoons lemon juice
50g/2 oz caster sugar
2 × 5ml spoons/2 teaspoons ground cinnamon
1 × 5ml spoon/1 teaspoon grated lemon rind

225g/8 oz blanched almonds, chopped
225g/8 oz walnuts, chopped
SYRUP:
350g/12 oz sugar
100g/4 oz honey
600ml/1 pint water
1 stick cinnamon
a strip of thinly pared lemon rind

Brush a 33 × 23cm/13 × 9 in baking tin with melted butter. Cut sheets of the filo pastry exactly to fit the tin. Place 1 sheet in the tin, brush it with butter and continue until you have about 12 layers and have used almost half the pastry. Keep unused pastry covered completely with a clean, damp tea-towel to prevent it from drying out.

To make the filling, dissolve the honey in the lemon juice. Stir in the sugar, cinnamon, lemon rind and nuts. Spread half of the filling over the pastry in the tin.

Cover the filling with 3 sheets of pastry, brushing each one with butter. Spread the remaining filling, then cover with the remaining sheets of pastry, brushing each one with butter. Brush the top generously with butter and mark it into diamonds, cutting almost through to the filling.

Bake in the oven at 160°C/325°F/Gas 3 for 1 hour, or until the pastry top is crisp and golden brown.

Meanwhile, make the syrup. Place the ingredients in a pan and stir over low heat until the sugar and honey have dissolved. Increase the heat, bring to the boil and boil for 10 minutes. Set aside to cool. Discard the cinnamon.

Pour the syrup evenly over the hot pastry. Stand the tin on a wire rack and leave overnight to cool.

Siphniotiki Pitta me Meli
Siphnos Honey Cake

Serves 8

For the true flavour of the region, use Greek Hymettus honey.

75g/3 oz butter, cut into small pieces
100g/4 oz flour
1 × 15ml spoon/1 tablespoon lemon juice
100g/4 oz full-fat cream cheese
4 × 15ml spoons/ 4 tablespoons honey

75g/3 oz caster sugar
2 × 5ml spoons/2 teaspoons ground cinnamon
2 eggs, beaten
25g/1 oz granulated sugar

Rub the butter into the flour until the mixture is like fine breadcrumbs.
Sprinkle the lemon juice and mix to make a stiff dough. Knead the dough in
the bowl until it is smooth and free from cracks.
Roll out the dough on a lightly floured board and line a greased and floured
20cm/8 in flan ring on a baking sheet.
Beat the cheese, honey, caster sugar and half the cinnamon until the mixture
is smooth and has the texture of whipped cream. Gradually beat in the eggs.
Pour the mixture into the flan ring.
Mix together the granulated sugar and the remaining cinnamon and sprinkle
over the filling.
Bake in the oven at 180°C/350°F/Gas 4 for 30–35 minutes until the filling is
set. Cool the cake in the ring, then turn it out on to a wire rack
to become cold.

Loukoumades
Honey Fritters

Makes about 30

These totally irresistible little fritters are sold in pastry shops and are just the thing for a mid-morning snack or to enjoy with coffee after a meal.

15g/¾ oz fresh yeast
300ml/½ pint lukewarm water
350g/12 oz flour
1½ × 5ml spoons/1½ teaspoons ground cinnamon
salt
6 × 15ml spoons/6 tablespoons lukewarm milk
2 eggs, beaten
oil for deep-frying

50g/2 oz caster sugar
75g/3 oz toasted almonds, finely chopped, to serve
SYRUP:
225g/8 oz honey
100g/4 oz sugar
150ml/¼ pint water
1 × 15ml spoon/1 tablespoon lemon juice
1 stick cinnamon

Sprinkle the yeast on to a little of the warm water and stir well, then cover and set aside for 15 minutes until it becomes frothy.

Sift the flour, ½ × 5ml spoon/½ teaspoon of the cinnamon and salt into a bowl. Make a well in the centre and pour in the yeast solution, the remaining water and milk. Gradually draw in the flour from the sides and beat in the eggs. Beat the batter thoroughly until bubbles appear on the surface.

To make the syrup put all the ingredients in a pan and stir over low heat until the sugar and honey have dissolved. Increase the heat, bring to the boil and boil for 10 minutes. Set aside to cool, then discard the cinnamon.

Heat oil for deep-frying to a temperature of 190°C/375°F, or when a cube of day-old bread browns in 50 seconds. Drop in 1 × 15ml spoon/1 tablespoon of the batter and fry for about 3 minutes, turning them once or twice, until the fritters are puffed up and golden brown. Keep the cooked fritters warm while you cook the remainder in the same way.

Stir the remaining cinnamon with the caster sugar. Toss the cooked fritters on kitchen paper to dry them, then roll them in the sugar mixture. Pile them on to a heated dish and scatter the almonds on top. Serve hot, with the syrup separate.

Honey Fritters

Glika Koutaliou
'Spoon' Sweets

Fills 3 × 450g/1 lb jars

It seems that every Greek household has a jar of preserved fruits to offer visitors, together with a coffee and a glass of ice-cold water. Serve the fruit on very small dishes with a little of the syrup.

1kg/2¼ lb fresh fruit, such as cherries, grapes, small figs, gooseberries
600ml/1 pint water
675g/1½ lb sugar

2 × 15ml spoons/2 tablespoons lemon juice
a strip of thinly pared lemon rind
2 drops vanilla essence

Prepare the fruit: stone cherries, seed grapes, top and tail gooseberries and so on.

Put the water and sugar in a pan and stir over low heat until the sugar has dissolved. Increase the heat, bring to the boil and boil the syrup for 5 minutes. Add the fruit, lemon juice, lemon rind and essence, then simmer gently for a further 10 minutes. Pour it all into a bowl, cover and leave it for 24 hours.

Return the fruit and syrup to the pan, bring to the boil and simmer for 5 minutes. Repeat this process once more. Discard the lemon rind.

Spoon the fruit and syrup into warm, sterilized jars, cover with screw-on or clip-on lids (jam-pot covers are not suitable), cool, label and store.

MENUS

Buffet Supper

A selection of popular Greek dishes, many of which can be completely prepared in advance, is a practical and delicious choice for a buffet supper party.

Smoked Cod's Roe Salad – Taramosalata (page 14)
Aubergine Salad — Melitzano Salata (page 13)
Stuffed Vine Leaves — Dolmathes (page 12)
Crudités (chopped raw vegetables) and warm pitta bread — Lahanika Kai Pitta

•

Lamb and Aubergine Pie — Moussaka (page 50)
Chicken and Egg Pie — Kotopitta me Avga (page 56)
Bean Salad — Fassolia-salata (page 77)
Tomato Salad — Domatasalata (page 73)

•

Greek Coffee — Elenikos Cafes
Nut pastries — Baklava (page 88)

Dinner Party

Flatter your guests with a menu that captures the flavour of Greece.

Salted Almonds — Amigdala Alatismena (page 11)
Mini Meat Balls — Keftedakia (page 17)

•

Squid and Tomato Soup — Kalamarasoupa me Domata (page 25)
Marinated Lamb Parcels — Arni se Lethoharto (page 49)
Baked Stuffed Tomatoes — Domates Yemistes (page 74)
Sauté Potatoes — Patates Tiganites
Leaf Spinach — Spanaki

•

Cream Pie — Galatoboureko (page 69)

•

Greek Coffee — Elenikos Cafes
Fig Sweetmeat — Siko Gliko (page 84)

Summer Barbecue

Nothing can beat the tantalizing waft of fish sizzling over a charcoal grill – perfection.

Cheese Triangles — Tiropitakia (page 16)

•

Grilled Fish in Vine Leaves — Psari sta Klimatofilla (page 41)
Garlic Sauce — Skorthalia (page 28)
Spinach Pilaff — Rizi Pilafi me Spanaki (page 71)
Greek Country Salad — Horiatikisalata (page 73)

INDEX